On Stage

Theater Games and Activities for Kids

Lisa Bany-Winters

CHICAGO REVIEW PRESS

Library of Congress Cataloging-in-Publication Data

Bany-Winters, Lisa

    On stage : theater games and activities for kids / by Lisa Bany-
Winters.

    p.   cm.

    Includes bibliographical references.

    Summary: Covers basic theater vocabulary, puppetry and pantomime, sound effects, cos-
tumes, props, and makeup; includes several play scripts.

    ISBN 1-55652-324-6

    1. Drama in education. 2. Play. 3. Children's plays, American.
[1. Drama in education. 2. Plays.] I. Title.

PN3171.B27 1997

327.12'32—dc21

                                   97-14018

                                       CIP

                                     AC

Interior design and illustrations by Sean O'Neill

First edition
Published by Chicago Review Press, Incorporated
814 North Franklin Street
Chicago, Illinois 60610
ISBN 1-55652-324-6
Printed in the United States of America
10 9 8 7

Dedicated to Brian, with love,
and to everyone who has ever played with me.
In loving memory of Michael Bany

Viola Spolin, author of Improvisation for the Theater, Theater Games for Rehearsal, *and* Theater Games for the Classroom, *first introduced the idea of teaching theater through games. She inspired many of the concepts and originated some of the techniques found in this book. She has been a great inspiration for me and helped to instill in me, at a very young age, a love for theater. As a child, I played many of her games without realizing where they originated, how important they are in theater, and how much I was learning. I only knew I was having a lot of fun. I hope that others enjoy this book as much as I have enjoyed the books of Viola Spolin.*

Contents

Theater in the Round (Games Played in a Circle)

Make 'Em Laugh (Ideas for Funny Scenes)

Creating Characters

Improvisation

Introduction

Acting and theater games help people of all ages focus and concentrate their energies and improve their writing and communication skills—tools useful in every aspect of life. *On Stage* is a book designed to help children learn by doing. They can expand their imaginations, free the way they think, talk, and move. They'll learn how to express themselves with their voice and their bodies.

Theater skills enhance children's self esteem, make it easier to step into new situations, help them problem-solve, strengthen listening skills, encourage cooperation, make interaction with others more comfortable, and manage public speaking fears. Although this book is listed for children between the ages of six and twelve, children as young as four or five can understand basic acting concepts. And anyone who is young at heart will have fun with the theater games and improvisation.

The serious performer, director, and drama teacher will find that all acting techniques can be taught through games, teaching a variety of performance, storytelling, and character-development skills. Games at the beginning of a class or rehearsal strengthen work with a script by helping actors warm up, focus their energy, develop their characters, work with each other, even memorize their lines.

Most of these games require few props and little or no advance preparation. Many games can be changed for more fun. Some ideas are listed following many of the activities. This section is called "Play it Again, Sam!" The first chapter of this book, "Getting Onstage," includes fun ways to teach some very important theater terms and basic theater concepts such as blocking and stage pictures. These will be of special interest to teachers or directors working with young children. The exercises in this chapter are excellent for early rehearsals or drama classes because they give performers the foundation for communicating throughout rehearsals and classes.

The second chapter, "Twisting Your Tongue and Warming Up," includes games that are great to do at the beginning of class or rehearsal or before a show to help young people prepare physically and vocally for performing.

The chapter called "Anytime Theater Games" is filled with games that are great for enhancing listening skills and fostering cooperation. Some of these games can also serve as ice breakers for students who are more shy.

The chapter called "Theater in the Round" is filled with games that are great for groups. They can be played standing or sitting in a circle. They make good party games or can be used as actor warm-ups.

These games help strengthen improvisation, memorization, and focusing skills as well as promote team building.

"Make 'Em Laugh (Ideas for Funny Scenes)" will give children a chance to develop their comedic skills. Creative writing teachers might find these activities useful because they help participants develop story lines and flesh out characters.

The sixth chapter, "Creating Characters," will help children do just that—help them flesh out how a character walks, talks, thinks, eats, and everything else that makes a character unique.

Improvisation is the focus of the seventh chapter. Here's where young actors can develop their thinking and doing skills in an environment where anything can happen. Because there are no props or scenery, you can create anything simply by saying it.

"Using and Becoming Objects" is precisely titled because here, students are given the opportunity to become inanimate objects like a chair, a hat, or a rug and they can also find new, creative uses for familiar objects.

"Creative Drama" shows how to use pantomime, puppets, or masks to tell a story on stage.

In the tenth chapter, called "Behind the Scenes," young actors will learn what goes on behind the scenes and offstage at every theatrical production. Readers will be introduced to the people who help make the magic on stage including the sound effects person, costumer, makeup artist, and prop master.

The final chapter, "Skits, Scenes, and Plays," provides a few examples of children's performance pieces ready to be used.

You can teach these chapters in order or in any order you want. The point is to make as much fun as you can in whatever time you have available. And remember, the magic of theater can happen on a stage, in a yard, or in a classroom. All you need is your imagination and the desire to have fun.

Getting Onstage

This chapter is about basic theater words and has games to help you learn them. The italicized words in this chapter, such as *blocking* and *cross* are used by professional actors and actresses in plays on Broadway, in your hometown theaters, and around the world. They help the cast and crew talk to each other about their jobs. You can use them in putting on plays at school, in your home, or anywhere else.

You can practice your theater knowledge with these games. **Blocking** and **Upstage Downstage** are games that explain the basics of movement *onstage* (the part of the stage visible to an audience as opposed to *offstage*, the behind-the-scenes, not visible part of a stage). **Stage Picture** reminds you to never turn your back to the audience. **The Directing Game** puts you in the director's chair and **Who's Who in Theater** explains everybody's important role in creating and performing a play.

You don't need a stage for theater games. Just pick an open space and decide where the (pretend) audience is sitting. Poof—instant stage! For example, if you're in your backyard, the audience can be where the door to your house is, and if you're in your classroom, the audience can be the desks.

And now, let's get onstage and discover the magic of theater.

> *Actors are called thespians named after Thespis, a sixth century B.C.E. Greek poet who is credited with being the founder of tragic drama and the first actor.*

Blocking

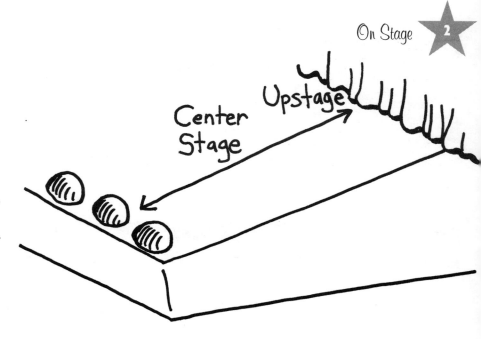

Center Stage **Upstage**

Blocking means where you stand and how you move onstage. *Stage directions* tell you where to go.

Upstage is the area on the stage that is furthest from the audience. *Downstage* is the area closest to the audience. *Stage right* is the actor's right, not the audience's. *Stage left* is the actor's left. *Center stage* is in the middle.

Why is it called upstage and downstage? In the nineteenth century and earlier, theaters had raked or sloped stages. That means upstage was actually higher than downstage, and the stage slanted down as it got closer to the audience. This made it easier for the audience to see everyone onstage.

In theater, the word *cross* means to walk like you normally walk. For example, you may say, "cross the street," while a director might say, "cross to stage left."

In a script, stage directions are usually written within parentheses and italicized or written on the right side of the page. Actors don't read them out loud, but they follow the stage direction instructions. For example, the script might read:

ALICE

I wonder what will happen if I drink this.
(*ALICE drinks from the bottle and grows taller.*)

However, the actor portraying Alice says, "I wonder what will happen if I drink this," and then performs the action described in parentheses.

Stage directions can be written in the script or you can get them from the director of the play. The *director* is in charge of the actors' movement onstage. The director also gets to *cast* the play. This mean he or she gets to decide who will play each part.

A stage direction or director might say, "cross from downstage left to upstage right." See if you can do this without turning your back to the audience.

The fourth wall *is a term used for the imaginary wall between the actors and the audience.*

Upstage Downstage

Two or more actors

Learning stage directions is an important first step to staging a play. Here's a great way to learn them so you can understand where to go onstage.

This game is best played on a stage. If a stage is not available, chose a large space and decide where the audience or downstage is located.

★ Props ★

Paper
Pen or pencil
Hat or bowl

Write the following stage directions on nine separate pieces of paper:

Upstage right
Upstage center
Upstage left
Center stage right
Center stage
Center stage left
Downstage right
Downstage center
Downstage left

Fold each piece of paper and place them all in the hat or bowl. Choose one player to be the director. The director pulls out a stage direction from the hat or bowl. The director reads aloud whatever stage direction he or she has pulled out of

Upstage Right	Upstage Center	Upstage Left
Center Stage Right	Center Stage	Center Stage Left
Downstage Right	Downstage Center	Downstage Left

Audience

the hat and all the other players must quickly move to the area that the director calls. For example, if the direction is upstage right, everyone must go to the back of the stage and to the right side when facing the audience. Then the director pulls out another stage direction and says "cross to _____" inserting the stage direction chosen. The other players cross or walk to that area of the stage, and so on.

   After a few turns, let someone else be the director.

Play it again, Sam!

Think of other stage directions to add such as:

   Face stage right and point with your upstage hand (Your upstage hand is the hand furthest from the audience.)

   Cross center stage and kneel on your downstage knee

   Cross downstage left hopping on your upstage foot

   Cross upstage center while facing downstage right

   Pat someone on the back using your upstage hand

The director can make the stage direction for only some of the people by saying, "everyone wearing blue cross to _____" or "everyone who ate cereal for breakfast cross to _____." *When you're playing with a group, see who can complete each stage direction first. See how many special stage directions you can come up with and add to the hat.*

Stage Picture

Three or more actors

This game is best played on a stage. If a stage is not available, chose a large space and decide where the audience is seated.

During a play, if the audience clearly can see everything, that means the performers have created a *good stage picture*. It's very important to face the audience and to make sure the audience can see everyone onstage. If you are blocking someone from being seen, or if someone is blocking you, that's called *upstaging*. The important things to remember in this game are:

Face the audience;

Don't upstage anyone; and

Don't let anyone upstage you.

Choose one player to be the director. The director tells everyone to walk around. The other players walk around the stage, going wherever they want, but staying where the audience can see them. At any time the director calls out "stage picture," and everyone must immediately freeze and strike a pose in a good stage picture. The director can move from side to side in the *house* (the house is where the audience sits) to make sure it is a good stage picture from any and every angle.

If the director calls "stage picture" and you have your back to the audience, or you are upstaging someone, or you are being upstaged by someone, you are out of the game. You must leave the stage, but you can help the director decide who's out. When ready, the director says, "walk around," and the game continues.

Acting tip for making a good stage picture: If you're downstage (see **Upstage Downstage**) you may want to kneel down so you don't upstage anyone behind you. And, if you're upstage, you may want to strike a nice tall pose, and be sure you're not right behind anyone.

Play it again, Sam!

Add more rules to make the game more difficult. For example, you can tell all players that their poses must be big and dramatic and everyone must smile.

When is it OK to cheat?
A director will often tell an actor to cheat out. This means to face the audience as much as possible, even if her character is speaking to another character on her side or behind her.

The Directing Game

Three or more actors

One of the jobs a director has is giving the actors ideas for how to say their lines and how to move onstage. This game lets you do just that.

★ Props ★

One chair

Pick one person to be the director and have her sit in the director's chair. Everyone else makes up a short scene—one that includes a lot of action. Here's one example:

Two kids are playing in the park, when all of the sudden there is an explosion. The kids faint. Another person screams and runs to get the firefighters. The firefighters come in, put out the fire, and wake the kids.

Once the scene has been created, the director calls out "places!" This means everyone goes to their place for the beginning of the scene. Then the director calls out "action!" and the scene begins. The actors go through the entire short scene and, when the scene is over, the director calls out "cut!"

Next, the director assigns all the actors a direction, such as "slow motion." The director then calls out "places!" and, once everyone is in place, then she calls out "action!" and the actors begin acting out the same scene but this time, they do it in slow motion. The actors continue to perform the scene until the director yells "cut!"

The director also can assign two directions at once such as, "slow motion and opera style." The actors act out the same scene in slow motion, and instead of speaking or making regular sounds, they sing like opera singers—even for the fire engine or police siren!

The director can even assign three directions at once, such as, "slow motion, opera style, while pretending to hula hoop." It doesn't take much to make this a wild and crazy game!

Suggestions for Other Directions

- Fast forward
- Overdramatic
- Doing the chicken dance
- Walking through Jell-O
- Laughing hysterically
- On one foot
- Under water
- Very nervous
- Backwards

You can think of a lot more!

Intermission *is the break between the acts of a play. During intermission the audience can stretch their legs or get a bite to eat while the cast and crew prepare for the next act. It's like halftime at a football game. Intermissions started when theaters were lit by candles. The candles had to be trimmed after an hour or so.*

Who's Who in Theater

From the first idea for a play to the final applause, there are all sorts of important jobs involved in creating theater. Each job is important and must be completed to create a successful performance. (We'll explore most of these jobs in more detail in Chapter 10.) Here's the rundown on who helps the curtain go up.

Producer: The producer is in charge of the business part of theater. He or she hires the staff and manages all the money, which means paying the staff, and making sure tickets are sold. Some things a producer might do to sell tickets are advertise in the newspaper and make posters for the play.

Director: The director is in charge of all movement onstage, other than dance. He or she casts the show, and blocks the play. The director will coach the actors in developing their characters in the beginning of the rehearsal process, and by giving notes about how to improve the play during later rehearsals.

Actor: Actors are the performers. They memorize their lines and develop their characters. They also get to take bows (called *curtain calls*) and get a lot of applause for their contribution to a play production. Boys and girls can both be called actors. (It's easier than saying actors and actresses all the time.)

Choreographer: The choreographer stages all of the dances in the play. He or she works with the director and musical director to make sure the dances will work well in the production, and then teaches the dances to the actors.

Musical Director: The musical director works with the director and choreographer to see that the music in the play fits in with the acting and the dancing. He or she directs the actors in the music for the play and is in charge of the musicians.

Stage Manager: The stage manager helps the director during rehearsals. He or she writes down the blocking so there is a plan of movement on paper and so that everyone can remember it. The stage manager writes up the rehearsal schedule, makes sure the rehearsal space is set up for rehearsals, checks all the lighting and sound equipment

When a stage manager is calling a light or sound cue, he says **warning** *about thirty seconds before the cue,* **standby** *about ten seconds before, and* **go** *when it is time to do the light or sound effect.*

The stage manager usually announces to the actors when it's five minutes to show time and she will call places when it is time to start the show.

to make sure it's in working order, and makes certain that anything the actors or director need is available.

During performances the stage manager calls the show. *Calling the show* means telling the light and sound board operators (see crew) when to fade or bring up the lights and sound throughout the performance. The stage manager is like a police officer who directs traffic backstage.

Designer: There are different types of designers. There are designers who make the sets, costumes, lighting, sound, props, and makeup. First, the designers meet with the director to come up with ways to make a show look and sound just right. Then they design or create their part of the show.

• The *set designer* creates the scenery—the background or setting for the play.

• The *costume designer* is responsible for what the actors wear. Costumes are important to help recreate the look of the time period. For example, if the play took place in a castle in the 1800s, it wouldn't be right for the actors to wear gym shoes.

• The *lighting designer* creates the lighting, which can set the mood or let the audience know what time of day it is.

• The *sound designer* is in charge of any sound effects or recorded music needed for the play. Perhaps the play takes place on a stormy night. The lighting designer could make the stage look like night time, and the sound designer could create the sounds of the storm.

• The *properties* or *props designer*, sometimes called a *props master*, is in charge of getting or making any items carried on the stage by actors. For example, in *The Wizard of Oz*, the witch's broomstick is her prop because she carries it.

• The *makeup designer* makes the actors' faces look like their characters. For example, by using stage makeup, young people can be made to look very old. You can also become animals or other characters with the help of makeup.

Crew: During performances the crew has a number of important jobs. The *stage crew* changes the set in between scenes, the *light board operator* fades the lights up and down, and the *sound board operator* runs the music or sound effects. There might also be a spot light or *follow spot operator* who shines a spot light on the actor who is speaking. These people are usually in the *light booth* where the light and sound board are located.

Understudy: The understudy is like a substitute actor. He or she learns specific parts so they can replace the actors who regularly play these roles in case an actor gets sick or cannot perform for some other reason.

It was the costume designer who suggested to Yul Brenner that he shave his head for **The King and I.**

2

Twisting Your Tongue and Warming Up

Just like athletes warm up before a game, actors warm up before performing, but they don't just warm up their bodies, they warm up their voices, too. It's very important that the audience understand every word an actor says so they can follow the *plot* (story) that is being told onstage. Practice speaking loud and clear and enunciating every word. *Enunciating* means pronouncing or clearly saying every syllable and consonant.

This chapter is full of fun warm-ups—some for your body, some for your voice, some for both!

You can try out **Tongue Twisters** with your friends or parents. Practice them and see how fast you can say them. Then warm up by shaking it all out with **Father Abraham**, a song that uses the body as well as the voice.

Energy Ball is an especially good transition game, for those times when you need a fun, quiet thing to do. You can pass the energy ball around while waiting in the doctor's office or backstage before your show begins.

Mirrors is a focus activity that gets players concentrating. **Number Game** is a focusing and listening game. It's a challenging game for people of all ages.

Warming up and concentrating on one part of the body at a time is called *isolation*. The **Isolations** activity is a great way to stretch out and relax from head to toe. Actors warm up their bodies so they will be ready to make their bodies become different characters or move freely—whatever a script demands.

Echo helps you learn about *projection*, which means to speak loudly. This is an important skill for the theater so the audience can always hear and understand you.

The last activity in this chapter, **Character of the Space**, is a way to get used to the space you're working in while, at the same time, help you get focused. In this game, you'll explore your environment while concentrating on different ways to move your body.

Once you warm up with a few of these activities, you'll be ready to get down to the serious work—and fun—of acting.

One or more actors

For stretching out your mouth and getting ready to speak in front of an audience, actors use tongue twisters to warm up. Try these tongue twisters. As you get better at them, try saying them faster and faster. Think of some tongue twisters of your own.

Start by saying this phrase ten times in a row:
Unique New York.

Repeat this phrase five times. Be sure to pronounce the consonants like the "*d*" in red, the "*ps*" in copper, and the "*ts*" in kettle, brittle, and brattle:

Red leather, yellow leather, copper kettle, brittle brattle, scadadilly dee (clap) scadadilly doo (clap).

Repeat this one five times:

A knapsack strap, the strap of a knapsack.

Repeat it five more times while snapping your fingers along with the rhythm.

Try repeating this one five times:

The big black bug bit the big brown bear and the big brown bear bled blood.

Here's a new twist on an old favorite:

Peter Piper, the pickled pepper picker, picked a peck of pickled peppers

A peck of pickled peppers did Peter Piper, the pickled pepper picker, pick

If Peter Piper, the pickled pepper picker, picked a peck of pickled peppers

Then where is the peck of pickled peppers that Peter Piper, the pickled pepper picker, picked?

Be sure to enunciate every "p."

You can find a lot of great tongue twisters in Dr. Seuss's books such as **Oh Say Can You Say** *and* **Dr. Seuss's ABC.**

The following sentence is for practicing projection:

Those old boats don't float.

Take a deep breath and hold each "o" sound. Pretend you're talking to someone across the sea, but don't strain your voice. Support it with your breath.

Father Abraham

One or more actors

Singing is a great way to warm up your voice. This song also warms up your body. That's why it's the perfect warm-up for just before a performance. Be sure to sing loud and clear and move your body, too.

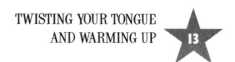

The song "Father Abraham" is based on a story in the Bible.

Father Abraham had seven sons, and seven sons had Father Abraham.

And they never laughed, and they never cried, all they did was go like this

With a left.

(Shake your left hand and keep shaking it while continuing to sing.)

Father Abraham had seven sons, and seven sons had Father Abraham.

And they never laughed, and they never cried, all they did was go like this

With a left,

(Shake your left hand.)

and a right.

(Shake your right hand.)

(Continue shaking both hands while continuing to sing.)

Father Abraham had seven sons and seven sons had Father Abraham.

And they never laughed, and they never cried, all they did was go like this

With a left,

(Shake your left hand.)

and a right,

(Shake your right hand.)

and a left.

(Shake your left foot.)

(Keep shaking both hands and your left foot while continuing to sing.)

Father Abraham had seven sons, and seven sons had Father Abraham.

And they never laughed, and they never cried, all they did was go like this

with a left,

(Shake your left hand.)

and a right,

(Shake your right hand.)

and a left,

(Shake your left foot.)

and a right.

(Shake you right foot.)

(Keep shaking both hands and feet* while continuing to sing.)

Father Abraham had seven sons, and seven sons had Father Abraham.

And they never laughed, and they never cried, all they did was go like that.

*To shake both feet without falling down, switch off feet—shake your left foot, hop on your left foot to shake your right foot, hop on your right foot to shake your left foot, and so on. Do it quickly to get the best warm up.

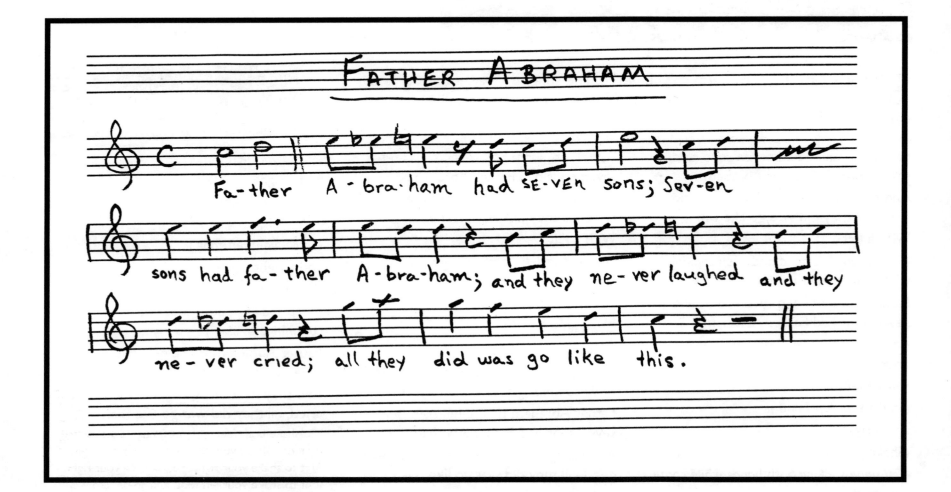

Energy Ball

Two or more actors

The curtain will go up in five minutes. You're backstage in costume and makeup, ready to go on. You're nervous and excited, but you have to be quiet because you don't want the audience to hear you. You can focus all that energy by playing this game using an imaginary ball of energy.

Hold your hands up in front of your face with your palms out. When you have the energy ball your fingers are tingling and moving quickly, like waving to someone. Look at someone else. Make eye contact with them, and toss the energy ball to them (just like tossing a real ball). Now their fingers are tingling and moving quickly until they toss it to someone else.

Toss the energy ball around and see if you can always tell who has it. When you get good at it, try tossing two energy balls around. When you get really good at it, you can even play energy volleyball.

I'VE GOT THE ENERGY BALL!

Play it again, Sam!

Start the game with everyone making a circle, eyes closed, stretching out their hands, and tingling their fingers all together, creating a big imaginary energy ball in the center. Think of sending all of your energy into the ball. Then someone picks up the imaginary ball and begins tossing it around.

*Play **Break a Leg Energy Ball**. Concentrate on sending good wishes into the ball, like the wish that everyone has a great show. Then, as the ball is tossed around, think of it as if it is carrying this good luck message to each person.*

Even some professional actors get stage fright before performing. Warming up is a good way to calm your nerves.

Mirrors

Two or more actors

Mirrors is a focus warm-up. It is a quiet game that requires a great deal of concentration.

Everyone chooses a partner. Each pair needs to decide who is player A, and who is player B. Stand facing each other, about two feet apart and make eye contact. Begin with player A as the mover and player B as the mirror. Player A should make slow movements with his arms, legs, torso, and face. While keeping constant eye contact with player A, player B acts like his reflection in a mirror, doing exactly what he does, at the exact same time. But player B can't look at the body part of player A that is moving—players must maintain eye contact throughout this exercise.

After a few minutes, player A says "switch" and, without stopping, player B takes over as the leader of the movement and player A becomes the mirror. After a few minutes, the new leader A can say "switch" and the roles are reversed once again. Do this back and forth a few times giving each player a chance to be the mirror.

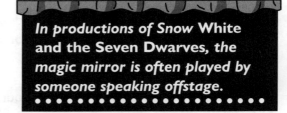

*In productions of Snow **White** and the **Seven Dwarves,** the magic mirror is often played by someone speaking offstage.*

Play it again, Sam!

*Play **Guess Who's the Mirror.** Someone goes out of the room while players choose who is player A and who is player B. Begin mirroring and, when the person sent out of the room reenters, she will guess which player is the mover and which is the mirror. Even when you say "switch," the change should be so smooth, that it is very hard for anyone to guess.*

Number Game

Four or more actors

Listening is an important skill for actors. They must hear what the other actors are saying in order to respond naturally, and they must listen to their director. It's easy to get distracted and start to think about other things. The Number Game helps actors develop their listening skills and helps them stay focused. Because you improve at this game the more you play, you may want to consistently start your rehearsals with this game. You may also want to put a time limit on how long you play because once you get started, it's hard to stop.

Everyone stands in a circle and counts off, remembering their number. The last person always begins, so if there are six people, number six begins by saying someone else's number (four, for example). Number four then calls out someone else's number (two, for example). Number two calls out another number and so on. When you hear your number, say someone else's number.

Sound easy? Wait, here are the rules:

Rules:

1. No pausing. As soon as you hear your number, say another number. If you wait too long, you're out.
2. Don't say your own number. If you do, you're out.
3. Don't say a number that nobody has, for example, if there are six people playing, and you call out number seven, you're out.
4. When you're out, you go to the last place in the circle, and become the last number. Everyone else gets to move

up one number. Again, the last person (that's you now) starts. The game gets tricky because everyone has to remember their new number and can't say their own number.

Here's an example. Let's say six people are playing: Lisa (1), Danny (2), Stephanie (3), Joe (4), Susie (5), and Brian (6). The game begins with Brian calling out number two. Danny quickly calls out number two. Danny gets out because when Brian called his number, he quickly called out his own number so he moves to the end of the circle and becomes number six. Stephanie, Joe, Susie, and Brian move up one number (because they were behind Danny), but Lisa keeps the same number (because she was in front of Danny). The new order is: Lisa (1), Stephanie (2), Joe (3), Susie (4), Brian (5) and Danny (6). The game begins again with Danny calling out number four.

Play it again, Sam!

*When you get good at playing the number game, it's time to add on. You can add on just about any kind of thing you like, such as ice cream flavors. Everyone chooses a different ice cream flavor, says it out loud, and remembers it. Now start the game again, only this time you can say someone else's number **or** ice cream flavor. For example, you may be number three and Rocky Road. If anyone calls out Rocky Road, you say someone else's ice cream flavor or number. But you must do it quickly, and you can't say your own! When someone gets out, they still become the last number, and the people who were after that player move up in number, but keep the same ice cream flavor.*

Flavors don't change. So now you might be number two, but you are still Rocky Road.

Next, you can add on something else in order, such as days of the week. Number one becomes Monday, number two is Tuesday, and so on. Now you have a number, an ice cream flavor, and a day of the week. You can call out any one of these things, but don't call out your own! If you get out, numbers change, and days of the week change, but ice cream flavors don't change.

You can continue to add on, switching off between things that stay the same, and things that have an order, and change when someone gets out.

Suggestions for Add-Ons That Stay with You

- Sound and movement
- Colors
- Cars
- Countries
- Lunch meats
- Fruits
- Vegetables
- Exclamations
- Footwear
- Famous people

Suggestions for Add-Ons That Have an Order and Change

- Months
- Numbers in Spanish
- Presidents
- Letters of the alphabet
- Planets

"I'll probably come out on stage, take one look at those three-eyed TV monsters and faint dead away."—Judy Garland describing her stage fright for her first television appearance in 1955

Isolations

Two or more actors

When an actor becomes another character, her entire body changes. For example, if you are playing a sad person, your body might be slouched to show how sad you are; if you are playing a peacock your body might be proud, and you would move like a bird. When you *isolate* a part of your body, you move only that part. Try to keep the rest of your body as still as possible. Isolations warm up your body, and help you prepare to become different characters.

One person reads through this exercise while the other players follow the instructions.

Close your eyes and take a deep breath. Relax and let it out slowly. Now you are ready to do isolations.

Isolate your head. Drop your head down so your chin is to your chest. Roll your head slowly to the left so your left ear is to your left shoulder, then to the right. Repeat three times.

Isolate your shoulders. Roll them up to your ears, then back, then down, then front. Reverse the direction so you are rolling them up to your ears, then front, then down, then back. Repeat three times. For a challenge, try rolling one backward and one forward at the same time!

Isolate your arms. Shake them out. With your arms outstretched to the side, make five little circles forward with your arms, then five little circles

backwards. Make five big circles forward, then five big circles backwards.

Isolate your hands. With your arms outstretched in front of you, shake your hands away from you and say "Good-bye, good-bye, good-bye." Shake them towards you and say "Come here, come here, come here." Repeat five times, getting faster each time.

Isolate your rib cage, right above your waist where your ribs are. Put your hands on your hips to help with this isolation movement. Move your rib cage from side to side without moving the rest of your body.

Isolate your hips. Make big circles by rotating your hips one way in a circular motion, and then the other. Repeat three times. Now make little circles with your hips one way, then the other. Repeat three times.

Isolate your knees. Bend your knees and move your right knee side to side, then your left knee, without moving the top part of your body. Try moving both knees at the same time. Do this three times.

Last but not least, isolate your feet. Shake them out real good, one at a time. Wiggle your toes then rotate your ankles. Do this three times for each side.

Take another deep breath, and let it out slowly.

In theater "break a leg" means good luck. Some superstitious actors think it's bad luck to say "good luck" before a show, so they say "break a leg."

Play it again, Sam!

To warm up your voice and body at the same time, add a sound effect for each movement.

WOOOOOOhhh

Echo

Two or more actors

This game works best in a theater or large room. The running in this game warms up the body and gives you energy; the speaking helps with projection; and the repeating teaches listening.

If you're in a theater, everyone needs to go to the back of the house (where the audience sits), and line up in the last row. If you're in a room, everyone lines up in the back of the room. The first person in line chooses a sentence. It can be any sentence you like, but it should be easy for everyone to remember, such as: "Jack jumped over the candlestick." The first person in line runs onstage (or to the front of the room), stops center stage, faces the audience, and says the sentence loudly and clearly so everyone else, in the back of the room, can hear "Jack jumped over the candlestick!" If everyone heard and understood the sentence, they repeat it the exact same way. Everyone should also copy the posture and movements of the speaker. If someone cannot hear or understand the first person's sentence,

they yell, "What?" and the person tries again. Once this person repeats the sentence, they run to the end of the line, while the second person in line runs up onstage or to the front of the room for her turn. The activity continues until everyone has had a turn. Then you can change the sentence and start over.

Play it again, Sam!

*Play **Name Echo**. For a first rehearsal or a first class, you can use this exercise to learn each other's names by making your sentence "Hello, my name is _____." Then you follow the rest of the rules to **Echo**.*

*Play **Favorite Line Echo**. If you're working on a play, each player says his favorite line from the play.*

*Play **Character Echo**. Keep the same sentence, but call out different kinds of characters. All players must then say the line the way they think the character might say it, including characteristic body movements and voice changes.*

Suggestions for Character Echo

- Cheerleader
- Monster
- Teacher
- Opera singer
- Nerd
- Movie star
- Witch
- Old lady

*Try **Emotions Echo**. Keep the same sentence, but call out different emotions such as happy, sad, angry, or scared. Players then say the same line, but with the selected emotion.*

Character of the Space

Three or more actors

An actor should always be familiar with the space in which he or she is acting. This activity helps you get to know your space, as well as warm up your body, and practice using your body in different ways.

PUDDING!

Walk around the space you're in. It can be a theater, a classroom, a living room, or any open space. Keep walking, only now pretend you're walking through pudding. Think about what it feels like and how your body would move through pudding. For example, you might move more slowly because pudding is thicker than air. After a while, pretend the space has turned into clouds. Think about what that feels like, and how you might walk through clouds. The space can turn into all sorts of things. Someone is appointed the caller and whenever she calls out, it will change the way you move.

In Mary Poppins *and* Peter Pan, *young performers have to act like they are flying in the air. How might you be able to convey the image of flying?*

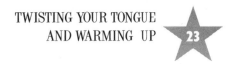
Suggestions for Different Kinds of Spaces

- Honey
- Snow
- Water
- Mashed potatoes
- Outer space

- Popcorn
- Wind
- Feathers
- Mud

- Fire
- Taffy
- Pea soup
- Tar

Play it again, Sam!

*Play **Shoe Character of the Space**.
Pretend you have on different kinds of shoes.
Whenever a new shoe is called, it will change
the way you move.*

Suggestions for Different Kinds of Shoes

- Roller skates
- Space boots
- Moccasins
- Ballet slippers
- Ice skates
- Tap shoes
- Tennis shoes
- Cowboy boots
- Cleats
- Motorcycle boots
- High heels

*Play **Color Character of the Space**.
Imagine what it would be like if you could
walk through colors. Think about what each
color means to you and how it makes you
feel. Whenever a different color is called see
how it changes the way you move. For
example, red might make you feel hot. Move
your body to show that you are very hot.*

3

Anytime Theater Games

Whether you're an actor or you just want to become more comfortable speaking aloud and thinking on your feet, you will enjoy playing the games in this chapter. They inspire creativity and will spark your imagination. You can play them just about anywhere and teach them to others. Many make great travel games, too.

Listening and working together are important theater skills. Actors need to respond to each others' words and movements, actors need to listen to the director, and so on. You can practice your listening skills with such games as **Talking Ball, One Word Story,** and **Grocery Store.** Cooperation skills are taught in **One Word Story** as well as **Machines.** Both activities will give you the opportunity to work with other actors as you create.

For ice breakers, try **The Attention Game** and **Change Three Things.** Even the shyest of people have been known to come out of their shell for **The Attention Game. Change Three Things** will make you carefully observe and study your partner.

The last game is this chapter is **Detective Handshake.** This is a dramatic and mysterious game. It's a favorite at parties and in camp groups.

Open up your mind, and have fun as you play these theater games anytime and anywhere.

In ancient Greece, plays often took place in the market place.

Talking Ball

Two or more actors

Talking Ball is a creative listening game and involves beginning improvisation. *Improvisation* (also known as improv) is a drama that is created on the spur of the moment, without any advance preparation; that is, you make it up as you go along. Talking Ball is a game that is the basis for more advanced improv games such as **Conduct a Story** (Chapter 5).

★ Props ★

One ball

Sit in a circle (or across from each other if there are two people playing). One person holds the ball and, while they hold the ball, they are the storyteller. The storyteller begins telling a story about anything. After a few sentences, the storyteller tosses the ball to someone else. Now they are the new storyteller. The new storyteller continues the story where the old storyteller left off. The second person must build off of the story that was started by the first person. After a few sentences, the ball is passed again and the story continues with a new storyteller. Keep tossing the ball until the story comes to an end.

You can only talk if you are holding the talking ball. You can toss the ball at the end of a sentence or in the middle. If the ball is tossed in the middle, the new storyteller continues the story exactly from where the first person stopped. For example, the storyteller may say, "There once was a dog named Rex. He had a friend named—." and then tosses the ball. The new story-teller completes the sentence: "Rover," and then continues the story.

Listen closely to the story, so when it's your turn to be the storyteller, everything makes sense.

Here's an example of how this game might work.

SALLY

(holding the talking ball)
Once upon a time there was a giant who lived on the moon. He was lonely, so he decided to build a spaceship to visit planet earth.
(SALLY tosses the ball to HENRY.)

HENRY

(holding the talking ball)
He built his spaceship out of cheese, but he didn't notice all of the mice who were spying on him. That night when he went to sleep. . .
(HENRY tosses the ball to COURTNEY.)

COURTNEY

(holding the talking ball)
 . . . the mice ate holes in his spaceship. They ate so much they couldn't move. They fell asleep in the spaceship.
(COURTNEY tosses the ball to SALLY.)

SALLY

(holding the talking ball)
When the giant woke up, he started up his spaceship. He didn't notice the holes. He landed in Switzerland, which was perfect because his spaceship was made out of Swiss cheese. He and the mice lived happily ever after. The end.

Play it again, Sam!

Going on a long trip? Play **Talking Tap**. Instead of tossing a ball when it's time to pass the story along, tap someone on the shoulder.

Much of history has been passed down from generation to generation thanks to the art of story-telling.

One Word Story

Two or more actors

This game is more difficult than **Talking Ball**. One Word Story is the basis for such improv games as **Dr. Know-It-All** (Chapter 5). Be ready to listen and think quickly!

Sit in a circle (or across from each other if only two people are playing.) Start telling a story, one word at a time, going around the circle (or back and forth with only two players). For example, in a four person game:

	AMANDA	
Once		
	JONAH	
upon		
	HANNAH	
a		
	DANNY	
time		
	AMANDA	
there		
	JONAH	
was		
	HANNAH	
a		

DANNY

little

AMANDA

cow.

Try not to pause. There are no wrong answers in this game. Just say the first word that pops into your head and see if the story makes sense. It's OK if the person after you doesn't say what you thought they would say. It's okay if you're not sure what the person before you is thinking. Continue the story until it comes to an end.

Play it again, Sam!

Think of three words that have nothing to do with each other such as shoelace, pickle, and Ohio. Try to use them in One Word Story.

Play **One Word Story Ball**. *Instead of telling the story in a circle, toss a ball to someone as you say one word. They say the next word in a sentence as they toss the ball to someone else, and so on.*

Play **One Word Story Energy Ball**. *Toss an imaginary* **Energy Ball** *to the person who says the next word.*

Try **Dr. Know-It-All** *(Chapter 5).*

Grocery Store

Two actors

Grocery Store can be a warm-up game because you must run while speaking clearly. It's also a quick thinking game that involves listening and using your imagination.

MILK!

★ Props ★

Two chairs
A wall with room to run about ten feet in front of it

Set the chairs about ten feet from the wall, with the backs of the chairs to the wall. Pretend the chairs are shopping carts. Each person stands by their shopping cart, facing the wall. On the count of three, the first person runs to the wall, grabs a pretend food item, loudly and clearly calls out the item name and then, as this person runs back to their cart, the second person runs to wall and grabs another food item. The game continues until someone gets out. But how do you get out?

Rules:

1. If you repeat an item that has been said already, you're out.
2. If you pause or take too long to name your item, you're out.
3. If you don't speak loudly and clearly, so your partner can hear you, you're out.
4. If you say something that cannot be bought at a grocery store, you're out.

Here's an example of how this game might work.

JASON

(running to the wall, pretending to grab an item, and yelling out)
Cereal.
(JASON runs back to the chair.)

EMALINE

(running to the wall, pretending to grab an item, and yelling out)
Hot dogs.
(EMALINE runs back to the chair.)

JASON

(running to the wall, pretending to grab an item, and yelling out)
Spaghetti
(JASON runs back to the chair.)

EMALINE

(running to the wall, pretending to grab an item, and yelling out)
Cat food.
(EMALINE runs back to the chair.)

JASON

(running to the wall, pretending to grab an item, and yelling out)
Milk.
(JASON runs back to the chair.)

EMALINE

(running to the wall, pretending to grab an item, and yelling out)
Cereal.

Emaline is out, because cereal has already been said.

Machines

Four or more actors

This is an ensemble building game. An *ensemble* is a group of people who work together for a common purpose. In this case, the purpose is to make a machine. This game will also help you overcome any fear you may have about feeling or looking silly. Just let loose and really become the machine.

First, decide what kind of machine you want to make. It can be a real machine such as a washing machine or a blender, or you can make up a new kind of machine, such as a monster machine or peace machine. One person starts by making a sound and coming up with a movement that is part of the machine. (Try to choose a movement that involves your entire body. Think about what kind of sounds the machine might make.) The first person repeats her sound and movement over and over, as if the machine were running. While she is doing this, the next person connects to her and creates his own movement and sound. To connect, you don't actually have to touch the other person, but make sure it is clear that you are part of the same machine. Once all the actors are connected to the machine, the machine begins to speed up. It gets faster and faster until it's going so fast that it breaks down, with all parts of the machine collapsing. Everyone falls to the floor, and the machine comes to an end.

The object of this game is to work together to make sure the machine gets faster and faster, at the same pace, and breaks down all at once. Be sure to keep your own sound and movement throughout the entire machine. Even though you are listening to and working with others, keep doing your own thing.

Suggestions for Kinds of Machines

• Pizza machine

• Telephone

• Laughing machine

• Computer

• Taffy machine

• Snow blower

• Human body machine

• Can opener

• Pollution machine

• Music machine

Some theater companies include the word ensemble *in their name to show that they are a creative group where everyone contributes to putting on a show and everyone's contribution is important.*

The Attention Game

Four actors

Even the shyest of people open up for this game. This game is so competitive you might not notice how well you're improvising!

★ *Props* ★

Three chairs
A stop watch or watch with a second hand

Place the three chairs in a row with an actor sitting on each chair. The fourth person stands close by and keeps track of the time. The person in the middle chair is called the listener. She has a very important job. The two actors sitting on either side of the listener compete for her attention by talking about interesting things or making funny noises. On the count of three, the actors on the outside chairs have thirty seconds to talk to the listener, at the same time. The goal is to attract the listener's attention. At the end of thirty seconds, the listener decides which of the two actors captured more of her attention.

Rules:
1. The talkers must stay in their chairs.
2. The talkers cannot touch the listener.

Play it again, Sam!

Play this game in front of an audience. Take topic suggestions from the audience and use these to try and attract the listener's attention. For example, the person on the listener's right might talk about sports, while the person on the listener's left talks about food. Let the audience help the listener judge who attracts the most attention.

Change Three Things

Any even number of actors

This is an observation and memorization game. If you concentrate, you will do very well at this game.

Everyone stands in two equal lines facing the other line. Your partner is the person standing directly across from you. Everyone plays this game at the same time. Spend a few minutes looking over your partner. Notice every detail from the top of his head to the tip of his toes—how he styles his hair, whether he's wearing a vest, are his shoes tied, are his socks up or down, and so on. After a few minutes, all players turn around, so they are facing away from their partner. Each player changes three things about themselves. It can be something as obvious as tucking in your shirt or as subtle as putting a ring on another finger.

After everyone has changed three things, everyone turns around and faces their partner again. Take a few minutes to look over your partner and try to figure out what three things have changed about them. Go down the line and see if everyone can guess what three things are different about their partner.

Detective Handshake

Six or more actors

Everyone likes a good mystery. This game lets you be the detective, the victim, and sometimes even the killer! You can practice being very dramatic with this game. Also your powers of observation are very important here—just like a good detective.

One player is selected to start. Everyone else sits down and closes their eyes. The selected player walks around the room and pats one person on the head. This person will be the killer. After the selected player has chosen a killer, she says, "Welcome to my _____ party." She fills in the blank with her favorite kind of party (tea, slumber, birthday, and so on). Next, everyone gets up and acts as if they are at that kind of a party. Everyone walks around the room and shakes hands with the other party guests. If the killer wants to kill someone, she gently scratches the inside of their victim's hand when she shakes it. The victim then *waits ten seconds* before dying a great, dramatic death. It's very important to wait ten seconds, and even shake other peoples' hands during that time, so you don't give away who the killer is. When someone thinks they know who the killer is, they make a guess, but if they guess wrong they must die a great, dramatic death, too! The game continues until someone (who has not been killed) correctly guesses who the killer is.

If you want to play again, the player who correctly guesses who the killer is gets to choose the next killer and the new kind of party.

Rules:

1. A guess cannot be made until at least one person has been killed.
2. The killer does not have to kill everyone who's hand he or she shakes.
3. You cannot refuse to shake someone's hand. If you think they are the killer, make a guess.

Don't forget to behave like you are at a particular kind of party. For example, if it's a tea party, pretend to be drinking tea as you shake hands; for a slumber party you can be setting up your sleeping bag; and for a birthday party you might be eating cake. Also be sure to die a great, dramatic death complete with sound effects.

Kojak was a television detective famous for having a lollipop as his prop.

4

Theater in the Round (Games Played in a Circle)

The games in this chapter are for groups to play standing or sitting in a circle. They make good party games or they can be used as actor warm ups.

Want to Buy a _____ is a memorization game. It can help you memorize your lines for a play, rehearse for an oral report, or memorize facts for a test.

People of all ages sometimes have trouble focusing their attention. **Zoom, Thumper, Guess the Leader, Pass the Clap,** and **Zip Zap Zop** are all excellent focusing activities.

Important basic acting and improv concepts (see Chapter 7) are taught in **Give and Take** and **Yes and**.

Listening skills are further developed in **This is a _____** and **Operator**—a favorite at indoor parties. These games require no set up.

Knots promotes team building and skills for working in groups—skills valuable in theater as well as everyday life.

Just like the gears of a watch or the parts of a machine, circles are for working together, everyone connected and cooperating with everyone else.

> *Sometimes theater is performed in the round. This means the audience sits on all four sides of the stage.*

Want to Buy a _____

Four or more actors

Memorizing lines is an important part of an actor's job. This is a memorization and listening game that can get really crazy.

Sit in a circle. If you are chosen to start the game, turn to the player on your left and say, "Do you want to buy a _____?" Fill in the blank with any object or animal that you think of such as a pig. The person next to you responds by asking, "A what?" and you repeat the animal name, "A pig." Then the person asks an *is it* or *does it* question about the pig such as, "Does it oink?" You answer the question with, "Of course it oinks." This second person then turns to the third person in the circle and says, "Do you want to buy a _____?" He or she fills in the blank with a new animal or object such as a car. The third person asks, "A what?" and the second person repeats, "A what?" You answer "A pig," the second person says "A car." The third person then asks an *is it* or *does it* question about the car such as, "Is it new?" The second person repeats his or her question about the pig, "Does it oink?" You say, "Of course it oinks." The second person answers the question posed to them with "Of course it's new." Now it's the third person's turn to ask the fourth person "Do you want to buy a _____?" and so on. Sound confusing? Just wait until you play it!

Here's an example of how this game might work.

ZACK
Do you want to buy a dog?

ANNA
(to ZACK)
A what?

ZACK
(to ANNA)
A dog.

ANNA
(to ZACK)
Does it bark?

ZACK
(to ANNA)
Of course it barks.

ANNA
(to JOSHUA on her left)
Do you want to buy an apple?

JOSHUA
(to ANNA)
A what?

ANNA

(to ZACK)
A what?

ZACK

(to ANNA)
A dog.

ANNA

(to JOSHUA)
An apple.

JOSHUA

(to ANNA)
Is it red?

ANNA

(to ZACK)
Does it bark?

ZACK

(to ANNA)
Of course it barks.

ANNA

(to JOSHUA)
Of course it's red.

JOSHUA

(to RACHEL)
Do you want to buy a fish?

RACHEL

(to JOSHUA)
A what?

JOSHUA

(to ANNA)
A what?

ANNA

(to ZACK)
A what?

ZACK

(to ANNA)
A dog.

ANNA

(to JOSHUA)
An apple.

JOSHUA

(to RACHEL)
A fish.

RACHEL

(to JOSHUA)
Does it swim?

JOSHUA

(to ANNA)
Is it red?

ANNA

(to ZACK)
Does it bark?

ZACK

(to ANNA)
Of course it barks.

ANNA

(to JOSHUA)
Of course it's red.

JOSHUA

(to RACHEL)
Of course it swims.
    Whew!

To memorize his lines, an actor may tape record the other character's lines, leaving space on the tape for his lines. Then, he can play the tape back and say his lines when the right time comes.

Four or more actors

Think of the sound a car makes as it's zooming by: "Zoom!" Now think of the sound a car makes when it screeches to a sudden stop: "Errrrr!" This activity lets you use your imagination, gets you focused, and helps you practice sound effects.

Sit in a circle and wind up an imaginary car. Make a winding up sound with your voice as you do this. Set the imaginary car on the floor in front of you, push it with your hand to the person next to you, and say, "Zoom!" That person pushes it along to the next person saying, "Zoom!" The car continues around the circle, "Zoom!" "Zoom!" "Zoom!" This continues until someone stops it by putting out their hand and making the loud screeching sound, "Errrrr!" That person changes the direction of the car, and pushes it the other way saying, "Zoom!"

When the car comes to you, you have two choices:

1. Push it along the same direction it is already going, and say, "Zoom!" or

2. Stop it by putting out your hand and saying "Errrrr," and then pushing it back the way it came saying, "Zoom!"

The only way to change the direction of the car is to stop it first.

If the car gets lost (if you don't know who has it or where it was last), start over by winding it up again.

Before theaters had curtains or lighting on stage, trumpets let the audience know when the play was about to begin.

Guess the Leader

Six or more actors

To be successful at this game you must focus, pay close attention, and observe everyone around you. Because this game requires no equipment and little explanation, it's a great transition game when you have extra time you didn't know you'd have.

Sit in a circle. Choose one person to leave the room while the remaining players chose another person to be the leader. The leader starts a movement such as patting her knees. The other players follow by mirroring her movement. The leader changes the movement periodically and everyone else in the group mirrors her action. The outside player, or guesser, comes back into the room and stands in the middle of the circle. The guesser has three chances to guess who the leader is.

The leader can choose any movement that the other players can do, too. For example, the leader can clap her hands for a while, then change to patting her head. Everyone continues to mirror the leader until the guesser correctly identifies the leader or has used up his or her three guesses.

For the next round, the leader leaves the room to become the guesser, and a new leader is chosen. Continue playing until everyone has a chance to lead and to guess.

Acting tip for the leader: Don't make any sudden changes in movement. Let the movements flow from one into the next so that everyone else can easily follow this change.

Acting tip for the guesser: Use your ears as well as your eyes. For example, when the movement changes to a clap, see if you can tell where the sound of the clap first came from.

Acting tip for the other players: Don't look right at the leader. If everyone is looking at the leader, it's very easy for the guesser to identify her.

Pass the Clap

Four or more actors

You can learn the basic concept of give and take with this activity while practicing rhythm too!

Stand in a circle. Turn to the person on your left, make eye contact with him, and clap together. The goal is to clap at the same time. Next, he turns to the person on his left, makes eye contact, and they clap together. Keep passing the clap around the circle. See if you can pass it in rhythm.

Be sure to focus and make eye contact as you take and give the clap. Always be ready for it, and keep it going smoothly around the circle. See how fast you can go.

Play it again, Sam!

Sing a song as you pass the clap. Keep the clap going with the rhythm of the song. "Take Me Out to the Ball Game" is a great song for this activity. Try slow songs and fast songs. Just remember to focus and keep the rhythm.

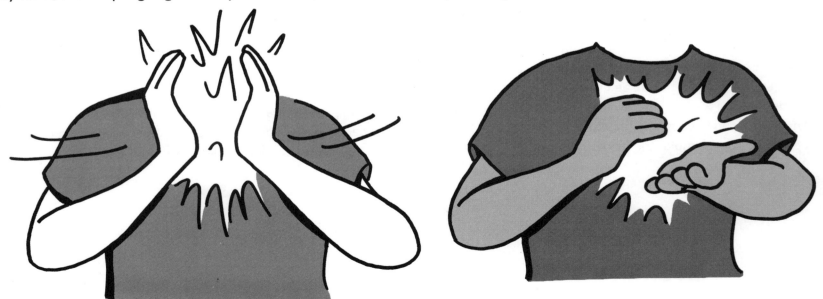

Zip Zap Zop

Four or more actors

This is probably one of the most famous theater warm-up games. Zip Zap Zop combines quick thinking with fast movements.

Before you play, practice jumping, clapping, and pointing at the same time. OK, since you can't actually clap and point at the exact same time, practice jumping and clapping and then pointing right after you clap.

The second thing you need to remember is the title of the game, in the right order: zip zap zop.

Stand in a circle. One person starts by jumping, clapping, and pointing to someone as she says, "zip." The person she points to jumps, claps, and points to someone else saying, "zap." The person she points to then jumps, claps, and points to someone, saying, "zop." The person he points to then jumps, claps, and points to someone saying, "zip," and so on The game continues until someone gets out.

Rules:

1. If you don't say the right word, you're out. Remember, it's always zip, zap, zop. Then it starts all over again with zip.

2. If it's not clear who you pointed to, you're out, so be sure to point directly at someone and make eye contact with her.

3. If you pause or wait too long when it's your turn, you're out.

When you're out, have a seat and help judge when others get out by breaking one or more of the rules. Continue playing until one person is left.

Play it again, Sam!

Play **Tongue Twister Zip Zap Zop**. Instead of saying regular Zip Zap Zop, say the words to your favorite tongue twister or song. "Peter Piper" works great. Just jump, clap, and point to someone saying, "Peter." The person you pointed to jumps, claps, and points saying, "Piper." The person he pointed to then jumps, claps, and points saying, "picked," and so on.

Four or more actors

Give and take is an important concept in acting. A good actor knows when to *give focus* to another actor, and when to *take focus*. If an actor is saying a line, all eyes and ears should be on her. When it is time to say your line, be strong and say it like you mean it in order to take focus. This game will help you learn the concept of give and take. It also helps you lose your inhibitions and not be afraid to get a little crazy.

Stand in a circle. One person is chosen to go into the middle of the circle and make a unique sound and movement. Repeating this sound and movement over and over, he goes up to someone else in the circle and *gives* them this sound and movement. To *take* a sound and movement, mirror the person giving it to you until you are doing it exactly the same way. When the giver is satisfied that you've imitated this sound and movement correctly, he will nod his head. The new person continues doing the sound and movement while moving into the middle of the circle. The original person takes this second player's place in the circle. The new person makes the sound and movement her own by slowly changing it into a new sound and a new movement. Then she gives the new sound and movement to someone else in the circle following the same pattern just described. Continue giving and taking sounds until everyone has had at least one turn. As you get better at this game, you can make your sounds and movements more complicated.

The title song from the musical Oklahoma *is the official state song of Oklahoma.*

Thumper

Four or more actors

WHAT'S THE NAME OF THE GAME?

Thumper combines the focus of the **Number Game** (Chapter 2) and the creativity of **Give and Take** (previous game) for a fast paced, competitive game. This is a great warm up or energy boosting activity for your theater group.

Sit in a circle. Pick someone to begin. He picks a short sound and movement that can be done from a seated position. He performs this sound and movement. Then the person sitting next to him comes up with a different sound and movement and demonstrates it. Continue until everyone has come up with and demonstrated their unique sound and movement.

To start the game, choose one person to be the leader. Together, everyone quickly pats or thumps the floor with their hands while saying the following chant:

LEADER

What's the name of the game?

OTHER PLAYERS

Thumper!

LEADER

How do you play?

OTHER PLAYERS

Fast and easy!

The leader makes her sound and movement and immediately follows this with any other player's sound and movement. This second player makes his sound and movement, then someone else's. (Always make your own first, then somebody else's.) As soon as somebody else makes your sound and movement, it's your turn. When it's not your turn, keep thumping on the floor. The game moves quickly, and continues until someone is out.

A real dog performed in the first production of Shakespeare's play Two Gentlemen of Verona.

Rules:

1. If you pause or wait too long when it's your turn, you're out.
2. If you don't make your own sound and movement first and then follow it with somebody else's, you're out.
3. If you don't get the sound and movement right, such as doing one person's sound, but another person's movement, you're out.
4. If you use someone's sound and movement who is already out, you're out.

When someone gets out, they stay in the circle and continue to thump, but that's all. Start each new round by repeating the chant. The game continues until there is one person left.

Play it again, Sam!

Play **Animal Thumper**. Everyone's sound and movement must be inspired by an animal. Here are some examples:

Flapping your arms like a chicken and saying, "bok bok."

Moving your hands like a snake and saying, "sssssss."

Holding your hands up like you're begging and saying, "arf arf."

Making your arms into an elephant's trunk and sounding like a trumpet.

Holding your hands up like claws and growling.

Yes And

Four or more actors

Supporting and cooperating with your fellow actors is an important skill, and the basis for acting and improvisation (see Chapter 7). To support your partner, *agree* with her ideas. Say yes to them. To *cooperate* with your partner, build onto her ideas. This game shows you how.

Sit in a circle. Make eye contact with someone and say a statement such as, "The grass is green." The player you made eye contact with then makes eye contact with someone else and says, "Yes," then repeats your statement, "The grass is green," and then says "And," and adds his own statement such as, "The sky is blue." The person he made eye contact with then turns to someone else and says, "Yes, the sky is blue, and clowns are funny." That is, each player repeats the phrase another

player passes to her and then adds her own. The game continues until everyone but one player is out. How do you get out? Here are the rules.

Rules:

1. Always say "yes," then repeat the other player's statement followed by "and," and then add your own statement. If you say "no" or "but," you're out.
2. No pronouns allowed. Pronouns are words like she, he, it, I, they, and so on. Instead of saying, "I like cake," use a name and say, "Lisa likes cake." If you use a pronoun, you're out.
3. Be sure to make clear eye contact. If no one can tell who you're looking at, you're out.
4. No pausing. If you take too long to repeat the statement or to say your own statement, you're out.

When you're out, leave the circle and help judge when others get out. Continue playing until one person is left.

Four or more actors

Discover working together in rhythm with this game. This Is a _____ becomes an intense listening game, because you must hear what is being passed to you at the same time that you must tell the next person what you are passing to them, and everyone is talking at once.

★ Props ★

Pencil, key, watch, rubber band, and so on
(You'll need a different small object for each player.)

Sit in a circle and hold your object in your hand. To begin the activity, every player turns to the player on their left and says, "This is a _____." You fill in the blank with the name of whatever object you're holding. Then turn to the person on your right and say, "A what?" Turn back to the person on your left and say, "A _____." Then turn right and say, "A what?" Turn left and say, "A _____!" Turn right, take the new object and say, "Oh, a _____!" Here you fill in the blank with your new object. Continue passing the objects around the circle until you get your original object back.

Play it again, Sam!

For a challenge, lie about what the object is. Pass a pencil around, but say it's an elephant. See if it comes back to you as an elephant. If you can't understand the person on your right, either say what you thought you heard or call the new object a "something" as you pass it on.

Acting tip: You are responsible for making sure the person on your left hears and understands you. That is your job. Don't worry about hearing the person on your right. They are responsible for you. If everyone takes care of the person on their left, the game will be successful. Just like in theater, if you take care of your scene partners, you won't have to be nervous because they'll take care of you.

Operator

Four or more actors

This is a quiet listening game that requires no preparation.

The object of this game is to pass a message all the way around the circle, so that it ends up being the same message as when it began.

Sit in a circle, and begin the game with one player whispering a sentence or phrase to the player on his right. That person whispers the same message to the person on her right, and so on, until it gets all the way around to the person on your left. The person on your left says the message out loud. You then repeat the original message out loud. If the message is the same, then you succeeded! If the message is not the same, it's funny to hear how it changed.

Rules:

1. If, for example, Emaline doesn't hear the message, she can say *operator* and the player sending the message must repeat it.
2. You may only say operator once. After that you have to pass the message along as best you can, even if it's not quite right.

Here's an example of how this game might work.

SOPHIE
(whispering to JASON)
The big green frog ate ten flies for lunch.

JASON
(whispering to EMALINE)
The big green frog ate ten flies for lunch.

EMALINE
(not hearing what JASON says)
Operator!

JASON
(repeating the message, whispering again to EMALINE)
The big green frog ate ten flies for lunch.

EMALINE
(still doesn't hear it quite right, but cannot say operator again, so she whispers to JOHN what she thinks she heard)
A big dog ate a bunch of fleas at ten o'clock.

JOHN
(the last in the circle, says out loud)
The big dog ate a bunch of fleas at ten o'clock.

SOPHIE
That's not what I said. I said "The big green frog ate ten flies for lunch!"
Well, they were close.

Knots

Five or more actors

This is a game for people who want to learn to work together on a play, team, school project, or anyplace where you're working closely with others.

Stand in a circle, reach your hands out in front of you, cross them at the elbows, and close your eyes. Everyone slowly steps into the circle and takes hold of the first two hands they come across. Once everyone has found two hands to hold, open your eyes. All of your hands should be knotted up. The goal is to unknot your hands, without letting go, until you're back in a circle. You might have to step over somebody, let someone crawl under you, or twist in any number of crazy ways. Work together to do whatever it takes to get back in a circle.

Play it again, Sam!

Try doing this without speaking out loud. With larger groups, have **Knot Races**. *See which team can straighten out their knot first.*

5
Make 'Em Laugh (Ideas for Funny Scenes)

Theater games can lead to ideas for a creative performance. In fact, theater games have been used by professional theater companies and improv troupes all over the world. The activities in this chapter as well as the ones in Improvisation (Chapter 7) will give you some ideas for creating comedy scenes. You can combine them to create a comedy variety show or comedy revue that your audience is sure to enjoy.

Conduct a Story brings a storytelling concert to your audience. You can let your audience participate in **Dr. Know-It-All** and **Gripes**. You can play guessing games with your audience in **Three-Word Skits** and **Syllables**. **Act a Joke** and **Commercials** are creative ways to develop original scenes for your performance.

Performing for others is exciting and fun. If you don't have a theater, you can perform in your home or classroom, and even one person can be a good audience, especially when you make 'em laugh.

One of the most famous stage mothers (a parent who dedicates her life to taking her child(ren) to rehearsals and sitting through them) was Minnie Palmer, the mother of the Marx Brothers. She went to their rehearsals and laughed at all their jokes. The musical Minnie's Boys is based on her story.

Conduct a Story

Three or more actors

After you have played **Talking Ball** (Chapter 3) try this game to create a concert of creative stories.

One person is the conductor. The other players gather together so they can see the conductor, some standing in back, some sitting in front. Just like at a symphony, begin by tuning and warming up but, instead of using instruments, use your voices. When the conductor gives a signal, such as lifting her arms, everyone warms up by speaking at the same time. Players can talk about anything they like, or just make sounds with their voices. The conductor cuts them off with another signal, perhaps quickly bringing her arms down. Now you're ready to start the game.

The conductor points to one player and he begins telling a story. At anytime, the conductor can signal to cut him off and have a new person continue by pointing to her. Each new player must continue the story exactly where the last person ended, even if he ended in the middle of a sentence or in the middle of a word. Try to make the story flow as smoothly as possible so that it sounds like one person is telling it.

Here's an example of how this game might work.

The conductor gives the signal for the musicians to warm up.

All musicians warm up by talking and making noises.

The conductor gives the signal to stop warming up.

The conductor starts the concert by pointing to Emma.

EMMA

Once upon a time, a little boy was playing in the yard, when suddenly he noticed . . .
(The CONDUCTOR stops pointing to EMMA and points to TESS.)

TESS

. . . that a flying saucer was flying over head. He watched as giant orange beetles flew out of the saucer, and landed . . .
(CONDUCTOR stops pointing to TESS and points to MARCO.)

MARCO

. . . in the little boy's sandbox. The alien beetles started playing with the sand, when the little boy said, "Excuse me, but this is my sandbox." The aliens said, "If you let us play, we'll teach you how to make a giant dino—
(CONDUCTOR stops pointing to MARCO and points to TESS.)

TESS

—saur." So they all built a dinosaur out of sand and called it Sammy. The aliens went home and the little boy got to keep Sammy for a pet. The end.

Notice how, in the last line, Tess had to finish the word "dinosaur," the word that Marco had started.

Dr. Know-It-All

Four or more actors

After you have played **One Word Story** (Chapter 3), try this game. Classmates, friends, and parents will especially enjoy the audience participation and the chance to meet a person who knows everything.

★ *Props* ★

Three chairs
One toilet paper roll or other tubular object (to use as a microphone)

Choose one person to be the announcer. The other three players sit next to each other, in the chairs, facing the audience. The announcer introduces the three as Dr. Know-It-All. The announcement might go something like this:

ANNOUNCER

I am proud to present to you the world famous, brilliant Dr. Know-It-All! Dr. Know-It-All knows it all! Dr. Know-It-All has the answers to all your questions. Let me demonstrate how brilliant he is. Dr. Know-It-All, what is two plus two?

Dr. Know-It-All—the three seated players—answer the question one word at a time, each person in order, just like in the **One Word Story** game.

AMANDA

Two

JONAH

plus

HANNAH

two

AMANDA

equals

JONAH

four.

The announcer then invites questions from the audience.

ANNOUNCER

Thank you Dr. Know-It-All! Now are there any questions from the audience?

The announcer calls on someone from the audience who asks a question. The announcer repeats the question, and then Dr. Know-It-All answers it.

Rules:

1. It's OK if you don't really know the answer to a question, just make it up. There are no wrong answers in this game.

2. Keep in mind that the three of you are playing one person. So, for example, sit the exact same way. If one part of Dr. Know-It-All changes the way he's sitting, all the players must change. Act the same way and take on the same attitude. If one of you acts like the question is silly, all of you must act that way. Try to make the answers flow so smoothly that it sounds like one person is talking.

3. Begin the answer by repeating the question. For example, if the question is, "Why is the sky blue?" Dr. Know-It-All should start the answer with, "The sky is blue because . . ."

Four or more actors

A *gripe* is a complaint. This is an improv game that gives you a chance to let off some steam. In this game, the conductor makes music by combining different voices and gripes into a symphony of noise.

Just like in **Conduct a Story**, the conductor stands in front of everyone else who gathers close by so they can see the conductor, some standing in back, others sitting in front. The conductor gives everyone a topic to gripe or complain about. (If you're playing this game for a performance, you may take suggestions from the audience.)

After everyone has a gripe, the conductor begins by warming up everyone. The conductor lifts his arms and everyone warms up their voices by making sounds and noises. When the conductor lowers his arms, everyone stops. Now you're ready to begin the game.

The conductor begins by pointing to a player. She then begins to talk about her assigned gripe. When the conductor cuts her off, she stops griping, but when the conductor points to her again, she continues what she was saying, from exactly where she left off, even if it was in the middle of a word.

Rules:

1. The conductor can point to one player at a time or many players at once.
2. The conductor can signal for the players to get louder or softer.
3. The conductor can signal for one player to get louder, while others get softer.
4. The conductor decides when to end the symphony.

Suggestions for Gripe Topics

• Cafeteria food
• Cleaning
• Homework
• Siblings
• Bad weather
• Broken toys
• Rude people
• Standing in line

Three-Word Skits

Four or more actors

This is a guessing game that is perfect for groups who enjoy performing for each other. This game can also help spark your creative writing instincts or help you develop a playwriting idea.

Divide into groups (or partners). Each group must come up with three words that have nothing to do with each other such as frog, telephone, and basketball. Next, each group quickly makes up and rehearses a scene that uses all three words, but they cannot say these specific words in their scene. When all the groups are ready, take turns performing scenes for each other. See who can guess your group's three words first.

Suggestions for Creating Good Scenes

- Interesting scenes have a beginning, middle, and end.
- Good scenes feature interesting characters.
- Plan the basics of your scene and rehearse it, but allow room for improvisation, too.

Part of the magic of improv comes from the surprises you can create in the moment.

Three or more actors

After you have played **Three-Word Skits**, try this guessing game. While usually played in groups or in front of an audience, this game can be played with as few as two players and one guesser.

With your group or partner, think of a three-syllable word such as *tornado*. Divide your word into syllables like this: tor-na-do. Your challenge is to figure out how to act out each syllable. For example, for *tor* you can act out the word tore; for *na* you can act out the sound horses make; and for *do*, act out the word dough.

Next, quickly rehearse three short scenes, one about each syllable, but don't actually say the syllable or the word in the scene. Going back to the example of tornado, your first scene might be about your homework assignment that your brother tore. Your second scene might take place in a horse stable. Your third scene might be about baking cookies. The scenes need to be performed in the order of the syllables. When you are ready, perform the three scenes for the other groups, audience, or guesser. After you have performed all three scenes, see if they can guess what your word is.

Acting tip: You don't have to act out the syllable exactly, as long as what you're acting out sounds enough like the syllable for the guessers to figure it out. For example, if your word is *yesterday*, you can act out *yes*, and use the word *dirt* for *ter* and act out *day*. If the guesser can figure out *yes*, *dirt*, *day*, he can guess your word.

Suggestions for Three-Syllable Words

- Elephants: act out the letter L, love, and fence
- Hypnotize: act out hip, note, and eyes
- Telephone: act out tell, love, and own
- Cantaloupe: act out can, tell, and lobe (as in ear lobe)
- Mysteries: act out miss, stir, and ease
- Manhattan: act out man, hat, and tan
- Paperback: act out pay, purr (like a cat), and back
- Porcupine: act out pork, you, and pine

Play it again, Sam!

Play **Pantomime Syllables**. *Perform your three scenes without using words or sounds.*

Two or more actors

ere's an easy way to make up comedy skits that audiences are sure to enjoy. If you have access to lighting effects, a *blackout* (where all the lights are turned off) is the perfect way to end these scenes. If not, ask someone to say "blackout" just after the punch line.

To begin, spend some time practicing telling jokes. Think of long jokes, jokes that tell stories, and jokes that involve different characters.

Choose a joke to act out. Decide who will play each character. (You can also add on to the joke so that everyone has more lines.) Decide on the blocking for the joke (see Chapter 1). Rehearse your joke until you are ready to perform in front of an audience.

Here's an example of how Act-a-Joke might work.

The joke:

Three people are driving through the desert when their car breaks down. They continued their journey on foot, traveling across the hot desert for days. Finally, they reach a palace. The sultan of the palace hears of their journey and calls them in. He says, "You three are very brave. Tell me, what did each of you bring that helped you survive in the desert?" The first person says, "I brought a large canteen filled with cold water, so we would not go thirsty." The second says, "I brought an umbrella to shield us from the hot sun." The sultan turns to the third person and asks, "What did you bring?" The third person replies, "I brought along the car door." "Why?" asks the sultan. The third traveler replies "So when it gets too hot, I can roll down the window!"

The act:
(*Three people act like they're driving in a car, suddenly the car jerks to a stop.*)

MADELINE
Oh no, our car broke down.

MAX
We'll have to continue our journey on foot.

WILL
But it's so hot here in the desert. We'll never make it.

MADELINE
We have to try.

NARRATOR
Three days later.

MADELINE
Look, up ahead. I see a castle!

MAX
Hurray!

WILL
We're saved!

MESSENGER

(entering)

I am a messenger of the sultan. He wants to know what you are doing at his castle.

MADELINE

Our car broke down.

MAX

We have traveled for days across the hot desert.

WILL

We are very tired and hungry.

MESSENGER

Come this way.

NARRATOR

Later that night, in the sultan's palace . . .

SULTAN

My messenger told me your tale. You three are very brave. Tell me, what did each of you bring that helped you survive the desert?

MADELINE

I brought a large canteen filled with cold water, so we would not go thirsty.

MAX

I brought an umbrella to shield us from the hot sun.

SULTAN

(to WILL)

What did you bring?

WILL

I brought the car door.

SULTAN

Why?

WILL

So when it gets too hot, I can roll down the window!

NARRATOR

Blackout.

The term slapstick comedy comes from farces (comedies with highly unlikely plots) that had characters hitting each other with a wooden stick for humor. It is used to mean very broad (not subtle) comedy.

Commercials

Two or more actors

Be the inventor, the writer, and the star in this creative activity. Use your commercials in between scenes of your play, or if you have access to a video camera, have someone videotape your commercials so you can see how they look on television.

Begin by talking about commercials and products people sell. Many commercials feature slogans and jingles. A *slogan* is a saying that helps you remember the product such as, "Silly rabbit, *Trix* are for kids." A *jingle* is a song that does the same thing. Create your own commercial by following these steps.

1. Invent a new product.

   One way to do this is to think of a need or problem people commonly have, and create a product that will solve this problem. For example, if you are always running out of juice, maybe you can make an invention that is part orange tree and part juice machine. It could make fresh orange juice whenever you want it.

2. Name your product.

   The orange tree and juice machine could be called the "Incredible Treechine."

3. Create a slogan for your product.

   For this combination orange tree

and juice machine, how about, "with the Incredible Treechine, you'll never be thirsty again!"

4. Create a jingle for your product.

Here's an example of a jingle that is to the tune of *The Happy Birthday Song*:

> The Incredible Treechine
> makes juice like a dream
> you'll never be thirsty
> it's the best thing you've seen.

5. Make up an entire commercial for your product using your slogan and jingle.

The Incredible Treechine commercial might go like this:
(MOM and SON are in a kitchen.)

MOM

Oh no, we're out of juice again!

SON

Why don't we get the Incredible Treechine?

MOM

What is it?

SON

It's part orange tree and part juice machine. It makes fresh orange juice whenever you want it. With the Incredible Treechine, you'll never be thirsty again.

MOM

Let's buy one today!

MOM AND SON

(singing)
The Incredible Treechine, makes juice like a dream, you'll never be thirsty, it's the best thing you've seen.

6. Rehearse your commercial until it's ready to be performed.

In the musical Annie *the song "Never Fully Dressed Without a Smile" pokes fun of radio commercials from the 1940s.*

6

Creating Characters

One of the most exciting things about theater is the chance to become someone else. One of the actor's most important jobs is creating and developing her character. Whether you are cast as a character in a play or are making up a character for a new scene, play, or story, it's important to give your character a life of her own. The way she talks, walks, moves, her personal history, even her favorite color, can be important for an actor to know about her character. The activities in this chapter are used for character development. These activities will help you learn to commit to your character while having fun becoming someone else.

The character most often portrayed in movies is Sherlock Holmes.

You can develop animal characters with **Duck Duck Animal** and **Poor Animal**—new takes on familiar games.

Today women can play men's roles. Glenn Close played a bearded pirate in the movie Hook.

How characters stand, walk, and move is explored in **Family Portraits**, **Through the Door**, and **Body Parts**. How they talk is explored in the **Sentence Game** and **Boom Chica Boom**. You can put all these elements together in **Short Scenes**.

The **Visualization** and **Hot Seat** activities are useful to fully develop a character, ready for performance.

Duck Duck Animal

Four or more actors

If you like Duck Duck Goose, you'll love this version, which lets you explore animal characters as you participate in a high-speed chase.

★ Props ★

Room to run

The setup for this game is just like Duck Duck Goose. Sit in a circle and choose one person to be the ducker. The ducker walks around the outside of the circle, patting everyone on his head as she passes, and saying "duck." When she wants to choose someone to chase her, instead of saying "goose," she names any animal she wants, such as an elephant. The player chosen chases her around the circle acting like an elephant, remembering to make the noise and movements of an elephant as he runs. The ducker runs safely to the elephant's place in the circle or is tagged and sits in the middle. If caught, the ducker remains in the middle until the

next animal is caught. The elephant now becomes the ducker, but he keeps acting like an elephant as he walks around the circle, patting people on their heads. The elephant continues around the circle saying "duck" until he chooses someone by saying another animal name such as "cat." The person chosen becomes a cat and the cat then chases the elephant. Everyone else in the circle should cheer for their favorite animal. Continue the game until everyone has at least one chance to be the ducker and chasee.

When you're picked, act like your animal the entire time, making the sounds and movements of that animal. Remember, some animals can run faster than others, some crawl, some hop, some fly, and some swim.

Poor Animal

Two or more actors

This game is about how funny animals can be and how hard it can be not to laugh. You can develop your animal characters and practice keeping a straight face with this game. Because it requires no set up, it's easy to play anytime, anywhere.

 Sit in a circle. One player goes into the center of the circle and tells everyone what animal he will be, such as a cow. He then goes up to someone seated in the circle and acts like a cow. He makes the noise a cow makes three times to the seated player, "moo, moo, moo." The seated player looks this animal in the eyes and says, "Poor cow, poor cow, poor cow," *without smiling*. If the seated player smiles, she must go into the middle of the circle and become the next animal. If she doesn't smile, the animal must try to make another player smile with his mooing.

The animal continues until someone smiles. If the animal tries everyone, and no one smiles, the first player who did not smile becomes the next animal. Whenever it's a new player's turn, they choose a new animal.

In the musical **Into the Woods** *the cow is played by a plastic cow (a nonspeaking role), but the wolf is played by an actor (a speaking role).*

As a young actor, Laurence Olivier—a famous stage and film Shakespearean actor—had trouble not giggling during rehearsals.

Family Portraits

Three or more actors

A picture tells a lot about a character—the way she stands, the expression on her face, the way she looks at others. This activity gives you ideas for different kinds of characters. It's as fun to watch as it is to play. If you're playing with a group, divide in half, so half can watch while the other half plays, then switch off.

In each group, choose one player to be the photographer. Everyone else in this group gets together and poses like they're having their picture taken. The first picture should look like a nice family portrait, perhaps some people are kneeling in front, while others are standing in back. Once you are in your family portrait position, the photographer calls out a kind of family such as "the musical family," and counts to three. The posing players have three seconds to change their position and pose the way the musical family would pose. For example, you might change the position of your arms and pretend to be playing an instrument. By the time the photographer is done counting to three, everyone should be frozen in their new pose.

The photographer calls out another family such as "the sleepy family," and counts to three. Again, the posing players change their positions and facial expressions to become the sleepy family before the photographer finishes counting to three. The photographer calls out four family types and then the next group takes a turn.

Suggestions for Family Types

- Crazy family
- Sick family
- Magical family
- Loving family
- Fighting family
- Goofy family
- Circus family
- Dancing family
- Rock 'n' roll family
- Gymnastics family
- Sports family
- Swimming family
- Movie star family
- Sad family
- Fire fighting family
- Artist family
- Aerobics family
- Lion family
- Teacher family

Remember, you are making a picture and pictures can't move or make sounds. Try to stay in the same place in the picture, so if you are kneeling in the front, you should always be kneeling in the front, even when the family picture changes.

Play it again, Sam!

If you have an audience, or are playing in front of a group, have the photographer take suggestions from the audience for types of families.

The SICK FAMILY

Through the Door

Four of more actors

Now that we have seen how characters pose in **Family Portraits** (previous game), the next step is to see how they walk. Everyone has a different kind of walk, and how they walk can tell a lot about a character. Here's a game that makes you act without any preparation time.

★ Props ★

A stage or a room with a door (Actors will need to be able to enter and exit through the door. The audience should not be able to see what's behind the door, but the actors should be able to hear through it.)

Choose one player to be the director. Everyone else makes a line backstage (or out the door or behind the screen). The director should not be able to see the players and should not know their order in line. The director calls out a character. It can be a famous person or a type of worker. For example, the director may call out, "cheerleader." The first player in line comes out and walks across the stage (or room) as a cheerleader. She may speak if she wants to, but the most important thing is to walk like a cheerleader. After she has walked across the stage or room, she goes back through the door and to the end of the line. The

director then calls out another character, such as "Captain Hook," and the next actor in line comes out as Captain Hook, walks across the stage, then gets back in line. The game continues until everyone has played a number of characters.

This game can get humorous because the players don't know what character they will be asked to play, and the director doesn't know who is next in line. The director may call out, "Snow White," and a boy may be next, or the director may call out "a mouse" and the tallest person in the group may be next. The player must give his best performance, no matter how different the part may be.

For ideas for characters, think of your favorite stories, famous people, or different types of work people perform.

The occupation most often portrayed in movies is a police officer.

The real person most often portrayed in movies is Napoleon Bonaparte.

Suggestions for Character Types

• Wicked witch
• Ballet dancer
• Robin Hood
• Librarian
• Mad Hatter
• Wrestler
• Pinocchio
• Scuba diver

Play it again, Sam!

Play **Reverse Through the Door***. Let each player decide what character he is performing when he comes through the door and have the director guess who he is.*

Two or more actors

Watch other people and notice how they walk and move. Some people walk with their shoulders swinging; others with their chests out. Here's another way to explore how different characters move.

★ *Props* ★

Room to move around

Walk around the room. Notice the way you walk, and the way others around you walk. Now walk emphasizing your head. Here, *emphasize* means to accentuate, to use the most, with the most energy. You can lead with your head or move your head around any way you want to emphasize it. Think of how it feels to walk this way. Think of what sort of character walks this way. For example, you might think the kind of person who emphasizes her head is a very smart person. Make up a name for this character. You might call her Professor Jones. Make up what this character does for a living. Perhaps she is a scientist. When you know your body movements and feel comfortable with your expression, introduce yourself to other people in the room. Go up to someone and say, "Hello. I'm Professor Jones. I'm a scientist." After everyone has introduced herself to everyone else, quietly walk around like yourself again.

Continue this activity emphasizing other parts of your body such as your chin, shoulders, chest, stomach, hips, or feet.

Sentence Game

Two or more actors

The next step in developing characters is figuring out how they talk. This simple activity lets you explore the voices of different kinds of people.

Sit in a circle. Choose one player to come up with a sentence that is easy for everyone to remember. If you're working on a play, choose a line from the play. Next, choose a character or type of person. The chooser says the line in character first and then everyone else in the circle has a turn, one at a time, going clockwise. After everyone has had a turn, the second player in the circle comes up with a new character for the same line. After performing it, each player performs it in the same order as before. Continue until everyone has at least one turn at choosing a character.

You can use this game to practice accents by picking characters from around the world such as a Southern belle, French chef, cowboy, queen, New York cab driver, or bullfighter.

Play it again, Sam!

Combine **Through the Door** with the **Sentence Game**. *Choose one player to be the director. He needs to come up with and tell the other players a sentence before they go backstage. When the director calls out a character, the first player in line enters, walks across the stage as the character, stops center stage, says the line in character, and then goes backstage.*

Boom Chica Boom

Two or more actors

Here's a song that works like the **Sentence Game**—perfect for practicing characters and warming up your voice. There's no melody, just say it in rhythm.

LEADER
Boom chica boom.

PLAYERS
Boom chica boom.

LEADER
I said-a boom chica boom.

PLAYERS
I said-a boom chica boom.

LEADER
I said a-boom chica rocka chica rocka chica boom.

PLAYERS
I said-a boom chica rocka chica rocka chica boom.

LEADER
Uh huh.

PLAYERS
Uh huh.

LEADER
Alright.

PLAYERS
Alright.

LEADER
One more time.

PLAYERS
One more time.

LEADER
(choosing a character or style)
Baby style.

PLAYERS
Baby style.

Now the song is repeated, only the words are spoken in character; that is, how a baby would say them. See **Family Portraits**, **Through the Door**, and the **Sentence Game** for ideas for other styles.

Short Scenes

Three or more actors

Use this activity to see how changing characters changes a scene and how different characters act with one another.

Choose one player to be the director, while everyone else chooses a partner. With your partner, make up a short scene where each actor says a few lines. Make the lines easy to remember because you'll have to repeat them and you're not writing them down.

Your short scene might go something like this.

JACK
Hello.

MARIA
Hi.

JACK
What's in your hand?

MARIA
Some candy.

JACK
I love candy.

MARIA
Do you want some?

JACK
Sure, thanks!

MARIA
Bye.

JACK
Good-bye.

Now the director assigns characters to each pair of actors. In turn, each pair performs their rehearsed scene using these assigned characters. Notice how changing characters changes the way the scene goes. In the above scene, sometimes Grace might give Jack some candy, for example, if they are girlfriend and boyfriend; othertimes, she might not, for example, if they are enemies. The director should give each pair three character assignments before the next pair performs.

Suggestions for Character Pairs

- Parent and child
- President and reporter
- Boss and employee
- Monster and witch
- Teacher and student
- Basketball player and fan
- Pirate and queen
- Movie star and director

Two or more actors

After you've performed many different characters, it's time to settle on one character to fully develop him. This is especially important if you are playing a character in a play. Use this visualization activity to explore your character's world. This is a quiet activity where you are thinking up answers and making decisions about your character without talking out loud.

One player can read while everyone else lies down on the floor, on their backs, with their arms to their sides, their legs uncrossed, and their eyes closed. Turn out the lights.

Now the reader is ready to begin. The following is written imagining a female character, but you can substitute the pronouns to make it work for a male character, too.

Think about your character. Imagine your character. Picture your character in your head and what she looks like from her head to her toes. Start with her head. What color is her hair? What style is her hair? Is it messy or neat? What color are her eyes? Does she wear glasses?

Imagine her face, her nose, and her mouth. Does she wear makeup? Does she wear earrings or a necklace?

Imagine the clothes she's wearing. What colors are her clothes? How do her clothes feel? Are they tight or loose fitting? Is your character big or small?

See your character's hands. Is she wearing rings or bracelets? Does she paint her nails? Are her hands clean?

Imagine your character's feet. If she wears shoes, what kind does she wear? Does she wear socks? Are her feet big or small?

Now think about your character's life. How old is she? Does she have a family?

Mary Martin played Maria in **The Sound of Music** *on Broadway.* **To help her get into character, she met the real Maria von Trapp.**

Does she have friends? A lot of friends or a few close friends? Is she married? Does she have a boyfriend? Does she have any children? How does she feel about her husband or boyfriend? Her children? How does she feel about herself?

Think about her favorite things. What is her favorite color? What is her favorite food? Does she eat a lot or a little? What are her hobbies? What's her favorite sport? What's her favorite game?

Does your character work? What does she do for a living? Does she like her job? Where does she live? Is it warm or cold? Is it a big or small town? How long has she lived there?

Now imagine that you are your character sleeping in her room. Imagine all four walls of the room. What sort of things are hanging on the walls? Is the room messy or clean? What colors are in the room? Imagine all of the furniture.

Open your eyes and pretend like you're waking up, as if you are your character in your character's room. Begin getting ready for your day. Imagine there's a full-length mirror in your room. Look into the mirror as you get ready. See yourself as your character in this mirror. Notice how you look from head to toe.

When you have finished getting ready, leave your home to go wherever your character normally goes after waking up and dressing. On the way there, stop at a park. Walk around the park. See something in the park that makes you sad. Go to the thing that makes you sad. See if there is anything you can do. Continue walking around the park. Now see something that makes you happy. Go to the thing that makes you happy. Leave the park and continue going where you were going. After your arrive at your destination, you may sit down.

Talk about the visualization. Everyone can share what in the park made them sad and what made them happy. Where was everyone going?

If you have time after **Visualization**, players can stay in character and continue with **Hot Seat** (the next activity). If not, players may "take off" their characters as they would an outfit, and leave them in an imaginary safe place where these characters can be retrieved next time.

Three or more actors

Once you're in character, it's time to let everyone else meet the new you.

★ *Props* ★

One chair

To begin this game, everyone needs to put on the character they created in **Visualization** or the character they are developing for a play. Place one chair at the front of the room. Everyone sits on the floor in front of and facing the chair.

One player begins by sitting in the chair. This player is in the hot seat. One at a time, the other players ask questions of the person in the hot seat. The person in the hot seat answers these questions *in character*; that is, answers the questions as the character would, giving responses that fit the character they are portraying. You can ask any questions you like. Find out as much about the character as you can. If you have done a visualization, ask them what in the park made them sad, what made them happy, and where were they going.

When everyone's questions have been answered, a new player sits in the hot seat and answers questions. Continue until everyone has had a turn in the hot seat.

Acting tip: If you're in the hot seat and someone asks you a question you're not certain how your character would answer, make up an answer. There are no wrong answers in this activity.

Oftentimes when a female actor portrays a character in a play who wears dresses, the director will tell her to bring her rehearsal skirt to rehearsals so that she can get used to walking, sitting, and acting in character.

7

Improvisation

When you do improvisation you act off the top of your head. Because nothing or very little is planned in advance, no scripts are necessary, and the characters and plots come from your imagination. Sound hard? It's actually very simple and a lot of fun!

One of the things that makes improv so much fun is that anything can happen. Because there are no actual props or scenery, you can create anything simply by saying it. If your scene partner is hungry, hand them an ice cream cone. If you're adventurous, go on a safari. The possibilities are endless.

Who, What, and Where, **Yes Game**, **Question Game**, and **Past, Present, and Future** will teach you the basic rules you need to know to become a successful improv actor.

The final fourteen activities in this chapter are activities in different ways to use your improv skills in scenes. Many involve taking suggestions from the audience—a wonderful way to get your audience involved in your scene.

> *Commedia dell'arte is a style of early improvisational comedy where the characters wore masks covering half of their faces.*

Who, What, and Where

You may have heard of improvisation in jazz music. In jazz, musicians improvise from a tune's melody and what they play is influenced by the other musicians. There are definite similarities between improv acting and jazz music. Both happen without much planning in advance. The musicians know the basic melody and improvise around it. Who, what, and where form the basic melody in improv.

Who:

Who you are, and what your relationship is to your scene partner(s), such as:

- Parent and child
- Salesperson and customer
- Teacher and student
- Boss and employee
- Movie star and fan
- Basketball player and coach

What:

An initial action to start the scene. It should be active, rather than just talking about something, such as:

- Building a sand castle
- Trying on clothes
- Taking a test
- Painting
- Watching a parade
- Learning to dribble a basketball

Where:

Where your scene takes place, such as:

- Beach
- Mall
- Classroom
- Office
- Street
- Gymnasium

Yes Game

Two or more actors

Play this game to discover the most important rule of improvisation.

 With a partner decide on a who, what, and where for a scene. Begin improvising your scene, but as you are acting with your partner, always say *no* to him. Say no, disagree, and negate your partner in every way. If your partner says, "Look at that elephant," you might say, "That's not an elephant, that's a rocket ship." If your partner says, "Let's go swimming," say *no*. Act out the no scene for a few minutes, so that you and your partner have both had a number of chances to say no.

Now start your scene again, keeping the same who, what, and where, only this time always say *yes*. Agree with everything your partner says. Build on everything your partner creates in the scene. For example, this time if your partner pretends to see an elephant, you might say, "Yes, he's the biggest elephant I've ever seen!" If your partner wants to go swimming, go swimming! Act out the yes scene for a few minutes, then bring it to an end.

After completing these two scenes, discuss which scene was more fun, had more action, and was more interesting. Chances are, in your no scene, you and your partner just stood around arguing, and didn't get to do anything; in your yes scene, you had the chance to do many active things. You might have seen an elephant, gone swimming, and more.

The most important rule of improv is *always say yes*. Play the yes game with your scene partner at all times. Working together in this way will make your scenes more active and much more interesting for your audience to watch. If you always remember to play the yes game, you'll be a successful improv actor.

Two or more actors

Play this game to discover the second most important rule of improv.

With a scene partner, decide on a who, what, and where. Begin improvising your scene, but as you're acting with your partner, you may *only ask questions*. You may not answer questions or make any statements of any kind including, "I don't know." Your scene might, for example, go something like this:

JAMAL

What do you want to do?

SALLY

Do you want to go outside?

JAMAL

Is it raining?

SALLY

How should I know?

Act out the question scene for a few minutes, so that you and your partner both have a chance to ask a number of questions.

Now start your scene again, keeping the same who, what, and where only this time, you may only say statements. Do *not* ask *any* questions. Also, remember to play the yes game. Act out the statement scene for a few minutes, then bring it to an end.

After you've acted out a question scene and a statement scene, discuss which scene was better and more interesting. Chances are, your statement scene was more interesting and went further than your question scene.

The number two rule of improv is *don't ask questions*. There are two reasons you should not ask questions in improv. First, you never have to ask a yes or no question because you are already playing the yes game. Asking the question just takes up time in your scene and is not active, so instead of saying, "Do you want to go swimming?" say, "Let's go swimming." Your partner will agree, and you'll be splashing around in no time. Second, asking questions puts a lot of pressure on your scene partner. For example, if you say, "What is that thing?" you force your partner to make up what it is. It's better to say, "Look at that lion!" and then your partner can talk about the lion to further develop the scene and move it along.

Past, Present, and Future

Two or more actors

Play this game to discover the third most important rule of improvisation.

With a scene partner, decide on a who, what, and where. Begin improvising your scene, but as you're acting with your partner, *talk only about the past or the future*—talk about what you will do tomorrow or what you did yesterday—but do not talk about what you're doing right now. Act out this past/future scene for a few minutes.

Now start your scene again, keeping the same who, what, and where, only this time *stay in the present*. Instead of talking about going to the mall, go there. Instead of talking about something you used to do, do something now. Also, remember to play the yes game and don't ask questions. Act out this present scene for a few minutes, then bring it to an end.

Once you've acted out a past/future scene and a present scene discuss which scene was better. Chances are your present scene had more action and active scenes are more interesting than scenes where the characters stand around and only talk.

The third most important rule of improv is to *stay in the present*.

Freeze

Three or more actors

Also called Stop and Go, this is perhaps the most famous improv game.

Two players start by choosing a line of dialogue and then begin to improv a scene that includes a lot of action. At anytime, another player can say, "freeze." The actors immediately stop the scene right where it is, and the two actors freeze. The person who said freeze taps one of the actors on her shoulder. She leaves the scene, and the person who tapped her replaces her, taking her exact position. The new player starts a brand new scene based on the position he is in. The other person in the scene goes along with the new scene, and the scene continues until someone outside the scene says freeze again.

Rules:

1. You must wait at least three lines before calling out "freeze."
2. You must take the exact position of the person you are tapping out.
3. The person who called freeze is the one who starts the new scene. The other actor must follow her lead.
4. The new scene should have nothing to do with the last scene.

Acting tip: This is an improv game, so don't plan anything in advance. When you see an interesting position, say freeze. Then immediately get into the same position and start a new scene.

Here's an example of how this scene might work.

(COURTNEY and DANNY begin a scene with the first line of dialogue, "I just love going to the circus.")

COURTNEY

(jumping up and down)
I just love going to the circus.

DANNY

Me too.
(pointing)
Look at that funny clown.

COURTNEY

(standing on tip toes)
I can't see. I can't see.

ROCHELLE

Freeze!
(COURTNEY freezes on her tip toes. DANNY freezes pointing. ROCHELLE taps DANNY on the shoulder. DANNY steps away from the scene and ROCHELLE takes his place.)

ROCHELLE

(starting a new scene, based on their pose of pointing, and COURTNEY'S pose on her tip toes)
You're a much better ballet dancer than that girl over there.

COURTNEY

(pretending to do a ballet dance)
I know, but I must keep practicing.

The new scene continues until someone calls freeze.

Cinderella *and* Romeo and Juliet *are two plays that have been performed as ballets.*

FREEZE!

Three or more actors

This game lets you explore many different kinds of acting and theater styles while you improvise.

Two players agree on a who, what, and where and begin improvising a scene. After a moment, another player, who is not in the scene, calls out a style of acting such as musical comedy. Without stopping the scene, the two players in the scene begin acting as if they were in a musical. After a few moments the player outside the scene calls out a new style, such as drama. Now the players immediately begin to act like they're in a drama. Each time a new style is called, the players change their style of acting, but keep the scene going. The players continue until the scene comes to an end.

You can come up with a number of different styles of acting from thinking about your favorite books, plays, and TV shows.

Suggestions for Styles

- Soap opera
- Science fiction (outer space) adventures
- Cartoon
- Tragedy
- Silent (pantomime)
- Sitcom (family comedy)
- Opera
- Talk show
- Horror show
- Shakespearean play
- Kung Fu movie
- Spy novel
- Music video
- Courtroom drama
- Documentary (educational)
- Foreign film
- Police drama
- Farce (broad comedy)

Play it again, Sam!

If you're working on a play, use this game to work on your script. As the actors run through the show, the director calls out different styles. The actors continue acting out the current scene but immediately change their style of acting.

*Play **Emotion Styles**. Instead of calling out acting styles, call out different emotions such as happy, sad, scared, excited, angry, or shy. Even if you're acting out a happy scene, if sad is the emotion style called, make it as sad as you can without changing the lines, but by changing your acting.*

The word tragedy literally means goat song because the ancient Greeks put on plays when they sacrificed goats.

Who Am I?

Three or more actors

You can tell a lot about people by how others treat them. Here's an improv guessing game that puts you in someone else's shoes. The trick is to figure out whose.

One player leaves the room or goes somewhere where he can't hear the other players. These players decide on one famous person for this exited player to be. The exited player is called back into the room and, when he enters the room, the scene begins with everyone treating him as if he is this famous person. Continue acting until he can guess the name of the famous person he is supposed to be. When he knows who he's supposed to be, instead of saying it, he should become the character. He lets everyone else know that he has figured out the identity of this famous person by doing things that this famous person would do. For example, instead of saying "I'm Michael Jordan," he might start a game of basketball. Once it's clear that he has correctly identified the famous person, the scene can be brought to an end.

Continue playing until everyone has a chance to be a famous person.

Three or more actors

Here's a chance to play your favorite celebrity. See how long it takes for others to figure out who you are.

★ *Props* ★

Three chairs or a bench

Set up the chairs next to each other so they make a bench facing the audience or the rest of the group. One at a time, three players enter the room, each acting like a famous person. They sit on the park bench and pretend to be in a park. They talk among themselves while each player trys to figure out who the other two famous people are. When one player knows the identity of another park bench sitting player, she lets them know while staying in character. For example, instead of saying, "You're Benjamin Franklin," you might say, "It's a good thing you discovered electricity." As soon as someone has guessed who you are, make up an excuse, in character, to leave the park. Then you may reenter as a new character.

Rules:

1. There can only be three people in a scene at one time.
2. Don't say who you are.
3. Remember the three rules of improv.

Four or more actors

Suggestions for Quirks

• You think you're a king or queen.

• You sneeze jewelry.

• You speak in opposites.

• You have an imaginary friend.

• You think you're a car.

• You're magnetic.

• You haven't slept in days.

• Your clothes are way too small.

• You have X ray vision.

• You're made of rubber.

• Every time you lie, your nose grows.

• You glow in the dark.

• Every time someone says the word "yes," you cluck like a chicken.

Remembering your rules of improv while trying to figure out what's wrong with the players around you makes this game very interesting.

Choose one player to be the host of the party and send him out of the room where he can't hear you. Three people play the guests at the party and each comes up with a quirk. A *quirk* is some peculiar or unusual trait. It can be as normal as having the chills or as crazy as having spaghetti for hair.

Call the host back into the room. The scene begins with the host getting ready for the party. One at a time the guests arrive, acting as party guests who have quirks—whatever quirk each guest came up with—added into their behavior. The host must figure out what each guest's quirk is by acting out the party scene with them. When the host thinks they know what a guest's quirk is, they say so in character. For example, the host might say, "Would you like me to turn the heat up? I see you have the chills," or "I just love pasta, do you mind if I try a piece of your hair?" When the host has guessed a quirk correctly, the other guests applaud and that particular guest makes up a logical reason, in character, to leave the party. For example the guest with spaghetti hair might say, "I have to go to the store for some tomato sauce."

The game continues until all of the quirks have been guessed correctly.

Play it again, Sam!

*Play **Party Quirks** in front of an audience. Take suggestions from the audience for quirks and ask the audience to applaud when the host guesses correctly.*

Superheroes

Four or more actors

Another party setting, but this time it's a gathering of crazy superheroes.

One person is selected to be the host of the party and three people are the guests. Decide on a world problem to solve, such as saving the rain forest. One at a time the guests arrive at the party. The host greets each of them by making up a superhero name for each and welcoming this character. Each guest immediately creates a character based on that name, and acts like that person. When all the guests have arrived, the host announces that they've been invited to the party to solve this specific world problem. While remaining in character, the group must come up with a plan to solve this problem, and then the scene must be ended.

The superhero name doesn't have to be based on a real superhero. Use your imagination to think of crazy names.

Suggestions for Crazy Superhero Names

- Frog girl (player must act like a frog)
- Screamer (player must scream)
- Opera woman (player must sing like an opera singer)
- Repeat man (player must say everything twice)
- Incredible jumping woman (player must jump up and down the entire time)
- Bird man (player must act like a bird)
- Boneless boy (player must pretend to have no bones)

In the television show Wonder Woman *Linda Carter had to act like she was flying in an invisible airplane.*

Hidden Intentions

Three or more actors

If you've ever wanted something, but been afraid to ask, you're not alone. In some plays, a character doesn't always come right out and ask for what she wants. An *intention* is what you want. In this improv game, you have to get what you want, without saying it.

Two players, named Elizabeth and Jonah for this explanation, need to decide on a who, what, and where for a scene that they'll create. Elizabeth leaves the room (or goes where she can't hear). Jonah is given an intention by a third player (Hannah)—something Jonah wants from Elizabeth, his scene partner. It can be an object, such as her hat, or an action, such as wanting her to tie his shoe. They switch places—Elizabeth comes back into the room and Jonah leaves—and Hannah gives Elizabeth an intention.

After both Elizabeth and Jonah have intentions, they begin acting out their scene. Throughout the scene, each of them tries to figure out what the other player wants, and gives it to them, but neither player can come right out and ask for what they want. When Elizabeth, for example, figures out what Jonah wants, she should make it part of the scene. For example, instead of saying, "oh, you want my hat," Elizabeth might say, "my hat would look much better on you. Why don't you try it on." After both intentions have been guessed, the players bring the scene to an end.

Play it again, Sam!

*Play **Hidden Intentions** in front of an audience. Take suggestions from the audience for the intentions and ask them to applaud when they are guessed correctly.*

Double Scenes

Four or more actors

Practice the concept of give and take in improvisation (see **Give and Take**, Chapter 4). It's important to know when to give focus to the other scene, and when to take focus back.

THIS COUCH WILL LOOK GREAT WITH OUR NEW CARPET

Divide into two groups. Both groups chose a who, what, and where that are somehow related such as a husband and wife picking out furniture at the furniture store, and two painters who are painting the couple's home. Both groups set up their scene next to each other. One group begins improvising. They continue for a few moments, until the other group takes focus by beginning their scene. The first group gives them the focus by freezing in whatever position they are in. The second group acts out their scene until the first group takes focus again, and the second group freezes. This continues until both scenes come to an end.

This game can get very funny because you can use what you hear in the other scene. For example, hearing that the painters are painting the house light blue and yellow, the actors playing the husband and wife could pick out furniture that is bright green and purple.

Suggestions for Related Who, What, and Where Scenes

- A mom and dad eating dinner at a restaurant, and a baby and baby-sitter finger painting at home.

- Two wives shopping for their husbands at a mall, and two husbands shopping for their wives at a mall.

- A dentist giving a dental exam to a patient in his office, and another patient and a nurse filling out forms in the waiting room.

- Two friends decorating for a party at the birthday girl's house, and the birthday girl and another friend listening to music in a car parked outside the house.

Storytelling Game

Three or more actors

The oldest known playwrights used a narrator to tell their stories. You can use this activity as a writing tool as well as an improv game. It will give you a lot of ideas for stories and characters.

To see how to create a play in the style of story theater from the **Storytelling Game**, read the scenes *The Tale of Jeremy Fisher* and *The North Wind and the Sun* found in Chapter 11.

★ Props ★

One chair

...AND THEN HE STARTED MOWING THE LAWN.

Set up a chair on one side of the stage or playing space, facing the audience. Choose someone to sit in the chair. This person is the narrator or story-teller. She begins telling a story that she makes up as she goes along. The other players act out the story as the narrator tells it. These players become whatever characters or objects the storyteller needs for her story and provide all the sound effects. Remember to give and take.

The narrator needs to pause from time to time while telling the story so that the other players can act out the scene she has just described. During her pauses, the other players take the focus and act out that part of the story then they freeze, and return the focus to the narrator to hear the next part of the story.

Try to play this game without planning anything in advance including who will play each part. When a narrator mentions a character, a player immediately jumps in to become that character. Play the yes game, so you are not arguing over the parts.

Here's an example of how this game might work.

NARRATOR

Once upon a time there was a duck.
(One actor immediately jumps in and becomes the DUCK.)

DUCK

Quack!

NARRATOR

The duck lived in a pond.
(The other players make the sounds of a POND.)
One day the duck noticed his reflection in the water.
(One player jumps in to become the REFLECTION.)

DUCK

Oh, look! My reflection.

NARRATOR

He didn't like what he saw.

DUCK

I look terrible.

NARRATOR

So he went to the duck beauty parlor.
(Players who were the POND now create a beauty parlor.)
A beautician gave the duck a feather cut.
(One player becomes the BEAUTICIAN.)

BEAUTICIAN

(cutting DUCK's feathers)
Snip, snip. There you go.

NARRATOR

The beautician told the duck to sit under the dryer for a while.

BEAUTICIAN

Go sit under that dryer.
(One player becomes the DRYER.)

NARRATOR

After a few minutes, the duck was ready to go.

DUCK

Thanks a lot! I'll see you later.

NARRATOR

And when he looked in his reflection this time, he liked what he saw.
(The same player becomes the REFLEC-TION again.)

DUCK

Much better.

NARRATOR

The end.

The story that has been remade the most times in plays, movies, and television shows is Cinderella.

Four or more actors

In order to understand what the actors are saying in foreign films, sometimes their voices are dubbed over so it sounds like they are speaking English, even though their lips look like they are speaking another language. When films are dubbed, the original sound is removed so the new sound can be added. This game lets you be the actors and the dubbed voices.

Choose two people to be the actors and two to be their voices. The players begin by agreeing on a who, what, and where. Each voice player stands near his actor player. The actors begin improvising the scene, without talking, but moving their lips as if they are talking. When the scene begins, the voices begin speaking for the actors. Remember to play the yes game in the scene, so that the voices go with the movements. For example, the voice should not say how sleepy the character is while the actor is jumping up and down.

Play this game at least twice so each player can be an actor and a voice.

In this game, both the actors and the voices have power. The actors have the power of movement. No matter how they move, the voices must play the yes game and make it work with the lines. The voices have the power of speech. No matter what they say, the actors must play the yes game to make it work with the movements. You can make a successful improv scene when you work together.

To celebrate the success of your production, you may want to have a cast party but, even though the name doesn't fit, be sure to invite the director and crew, too.

Gibberish

Two or more actors

Talking *gibberish* means mumbling or creating your own language, with sounds and words that you make up. Try having a conversation with someone in gibberish. See if you can understand each other by the way you say things—the emphasis that you place on each word—rather than the actual words you say. After you have practiced speaking gibberish, try this improv scene.

Choose a partner and agree on a who, what, and where. Your scene should involve teaching others how to do or make something. Give the title of your scene before you perform it. It should be in the form "how to _____"; for example, "how to bake cookies." Decide who will speak gibberish and who will interpret, or restate what the other is saying in English. Do not plan anything else in advance. Begin your scene with the person speaking gibberish explaining how to bake cookies, pausing every couple of sentences so the interpreter can restate what's being said in English. Play the yes game so that the English translation goes with the gibberish. Continue the scene until you have finished explaining how to bake cookies.

Suggestions for How-to Scenes

- How to tie your shoe
- How to swim
- How to ride a bicycle
- How to make a peanut butter and jelly sandwich
- How to change a light bulb
- How to change a tire
- How to fix a broken doll

Play it again, Sam!

Play Gibberish, *but this time the interpreter doesn't speak. Instead, she acts out what the other player is saying in gibberish.*

Slide Show

Three or more actors

If you've ever sat through a slide show of someone else's vacation, you know how boring it can be. Here's a way to make it very interesting.

 One person is the presenter; everyone else is part of the slide show. The presenter begins telling the story of her vacation. Throughout the story, the presenter says, "next slide, please." The other players strike a pose just like people in a photo from a vacation. The presenter uses this group pose to tell a story. The players keep their pose, as if they are an actual slide, until the presenter says, "next slide, please." Then the players change their pose, and the presenter continues the story of her vacation, explaining this new pose as if it were the very next slide from her vacation.

The presenter can set up how the players will pose by saying something like, "in my next slide you will see us climbing the mountain. Next slide please," and the players pose as if they are climbing a mountain. Or the presenter can let the players create a picture on their own by giving the next slide no introduction. In this case, the presenter must somehow work this new pose into the story. Continue the scene until the presenter has finished the story of her vacation.

THEN WE WENT MOUNTAIN CLIMBING

Keyword

Three or more actors

Here's an improv scene with a twist to keep you on your feet.

In a group, choose a who, what, and where. Each player in the group chooses a word such as *snake*, *bus*, and *together* that is related to the who, what, and where chosen. Begin improvising your scene. Whenever your word is said, if you are onstage, exit, and if you are offstage, enter. (If you're not playing on a stage, leave the scene; reenter the scene when your word is said.) You must exit and enter in character. Be sure to make up a good reason to exit or enter each time your word is said. You can have a lot of fun sending your scene partners in and out by working their word into the scene, but don't forget, they can do the same to you. Continue with the game until your scene comes to an end.

Here's an example of how this game might work.

Emaline's word is snake, Jason's word is bus, and Zack's word is together. Their who, what, and where is three friends making cookies in a kitchen.

EMALINE

I can't wait to eat all of the cookies we're baking.

JASON

Me too, and I'm so glad we could all get together for once.

ZACK

Oh no, we're out of sugar. I'll go borrow some from next door.
(*ZACK exits because the word together was said.*)

JASON

Let's cut the cookies into shapes.

EMALINE

Great idea. I'll make mine shaped like a bus.

JASON

I'd better go see what's taking our friend so long with the sugar.
(*JASON exits because bus was said.*)

EMALINE

(*calling offstage*)
Hurry up you guys! I thought we were baking together!

ZACK

(*ZACK reenters because together was said.*)
Well, they didn't have any sugar, but they showed me their cool new pet snake.

EMALINE

Look at the time. I've got to go catch my bus. See you later.
(*EMALINE exits because snake was said.*)

JASON

(*JASON reenters because bus was said.*)
No sugar. Oh, well, so much for making cookies. I guess we'll try again tomorrow.
End of scene.

The Alphabet Game

Two or more actors

Here's an improv scene with a challenging twist that will make you think before you speak.

With a scene partner, choose a who, what, and where. The first line of your scene must start with the letter A. The second line of your scene must start with the letter B, and so on throughout the alphabet. As you improvise your scene, each line must start with the next letter of the alphabet. If you have trouble remembering where you are, and if you have a third player, you can have him call out the next letter after each line of dialogue. Your scene should end when you get to the letter Z.

Here's an example of how this game might work. The who, what, and where is two zookeepers cleaning a cage at the zoo.

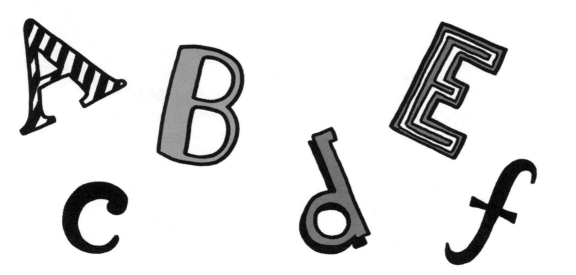

SOPHIE
All night we have to clean, clean, clean.

JOSHUA
Boy, you said it.

SOPHIE
Cages smell like animals.

JOSHUA
Don't even think about it.

SOPHIE
Elephants smell the worse.

JOSHUA
Forget about the smell. Let's get to work.

SOPHIE
Great, the ape's cage is almost finished.

JOSHUA
Hope they don't wake up while we're in here.

SOPHIE
I have to finish scrubbing the floor.

JOSHUA
Just do it quietly or they'll wake up.

SOPHIE

Kind of scary being in here at night.

JOSHUA

Look at that monkey snoring.

SOPHIE

My, he's filthy. Let's clean him.

JOSHUA

Nobody said we had to clean the monkeys.

SOPHIE

Of course not, but he's so dirty.

JOSHUA

Perhaps if we just give him a little shower.

SOPHIE

Quietly turn on the hose.

JOSHUA

Ready.
(JOSHUA turns on the hose.)
It's on.

SOPHIE

Splash water on him.

JOSHUA

(JOSHUA showers the monkey.)
That's better. Now he's clean.

SOPHIE

(pointing)
Up there is a monkey walking across the rope.

JOSHUA

Very hard for that monkey to keep her balance.

SOPHIE

Wonder what happens if she falls.

JOSHUA

X rays will be needed.

SOPHIE

Yes. We'd better call for help.

JOSHUA

Zebra cage can wait until later.
The end.

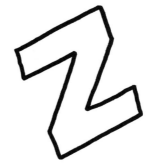

8

Using and Becoming Objects

In Chapter 6, Creating Characters, you learned how to become many different kinds of animals and people. In this chapter you can learn how to become objects. Things that aren't alive, such as furniture and musical instruments, are brought to life in **My Morning**, **Use or Become**, and **Human Orchestra**.

You can also use your imagination to find many different uses for everyday objects when you are acting. **Object Game**, **Someone Else's Hands**, and **Scarves** are activities that let you explore objects in new ways.

Becoming objects, sometimes called *object transformation*, and using objects in new ways expands creativity, both onstage and offstage.

*In the play **You're A Good Man, Charlie Brown**, Snoopy pretends his dog house is a fighting jet plane.*

The tornado in Wizard of Oz was created by swirling a silk stocking in front of the camera.

Three or more actors

Use your body to create everyday objects. Put them all together for an unusual and interesting scene. This activity works best with a large group, but players in smaller groups can play more than one object.

Talk about the objects in a bedroom, such as furniture, windows, and doors. Each player decides on one object in the bedroom she would like to play. (Larger objects may be played by more than one player.) After everyone has chosen an object, one player goes up to every other player and uses them. For example, if someone is a window, open them up. If someone is the bed, lie down on them. Do the same thing with the bathroom, the kitchen, and the living room.

Once you've created and practiced each room, put them all together in a story entitled "My Morning." Start by having everyone recreate the bedroom objects again. Wake up in your bed with your alarm clock going off. Turn off your alarm clock and gather your clothes for the day. Continue getting ready, but be sure to use all of the objects in the bedroom. Next, go to the bathroom. Everyone quickly recreates their object in the bathroom. Look in the mirror and brush your teeth. Take a bath or shower and get dressed. Use all of the objects in the bathroom. Next go to the kitchen. Everyone quickly recreates their object in the kitchen. The storyteller can make breakfast and sit at the kitchen table. Try and use all the kitchen appliances while making breakfast so that everyone has a chance to perform. Finally, go to the living room. Sit on a chair or couch and read a book or listen to music. Use all of the living room objects. Then bring the story of your morning to an end.

Play this game a few times so couple of players can act out their morning.

> *In Chapter 11 you'll find a version of* **Rapunzel** *that features an actor playing a radish. On the television show* **Pee Wee's Playhouse** *characters included* **Chairy,** *the talking chair, and* **Floory,** *the talking floor.*

Use or Become

Two or more actors

Become an object or use pantomime (see Chapter 10) in this fast-paced activity.

Choose one person to be the object caller. Everyone else begins the game by walking around the room. The caller names an object. The walking players have two choices—they may either use the object or become the object. They must do so immediately, without pausing. As soon as everyone is using or has become the object, the caller tells them to walk around again. After a few seconds, the caller needs to name another object for the other players to use or become.

Continue the activity until everyone has used or become a number of different objects.

Suggestions for Objects to Use or Become

- Washing machine
- Guitar
- Computer
- Light bulb
- Camera
- Motorcycle
- Napkin
- Scissors
- Vacuum cleaner

Play it again, Sam!

*Play **Partner Use or Become**. Everyone walks around the room on their own, but when an object is called each player must immediately match up with a partner. For each pair, one player must become the object and the other one must use it.*

Human Orchestra

Four or more actors

In this game, you can become instruments and create a full symphony using only your body and your voice. This game is similar to **Conduct a Story**.

Choose one person to be the conductor. Everyone else chooses an instrument that they will become. Once everyone has selected their imaginary instrument, all the orchestra members gather together, so they can see the conductor, some standing in back and others sitting in front.

The conductor begins by warming everyone up. The conductor lifts her arms and everyone warms up by making the sound of their instrument, as if they are tuning up a real instrument. As players make the sound of their instrument, they also move their body like their instrument moves when it is played. Everyone must stop tuning up when the conductor lowers her arms. Now the concert is ready to begin.

The conductor creates a symphony by pointing to different instruments at different times and signaling when the instruments should get louder or softer. The concert continues until the conductor brings it to an end.

You may decide on a song to play before starting the concert or you can make it up as you go.

Play it again, Sam!

Play **Partner Human Orchestra**. Here, everyone must choose a partner. In pairs, one player is the instrument while the other is the musician. Play this version at least twice so that each player can act in both roles.

Object Game

Three or more actors

When you look at a hair brush, do you see a microphone? This competitive game has you using everyday objects in unusual ways.

★ Props ★

Three or more everyday objects

Choose one person to be the judge. The remaining players divide into two groups, team A and team B. The two teams stand across from each other and turn their backs to the judge. The judge places an everyday object in the middle of the two groups. She then claps her hands to let the two teams know they may turn around. As soon as they turn around, a player from team A runs to the object and uses it in a way that it is not usually used. For example, if the object is a wooden spoon, they might use it as a guitar. The judge tries to guess how the player is using the object. As soon as the judge guesses correctly, that player runs back to his team, and a player from team B runs to the object. She uses it in a different way, such as a toothbrush. As soon as the judge says "toothbrush," this player runs back to her team, and it's team A's turn again. The game continues with the same object until one team cannot come up with a new use for the object. When this happens, the other team is declared the winner of that round. Play at least three rounds with three different objects.

Rules:

1. No pausing. As soon as team A is done, it's team B's turn.
2. No repeating. Once an object has been used as a hairbrush, for example, it cannot be used as a brush or comb of any kind.
3. Do a good job at using the object. If the judge cannot tell what you are using it as after a few seconds, your team looses the round.

Comedy sports *involves improvisational teams competing against each other.*

Someone Else's Hands

Three actors

★ Props ★

Table
Objects that can be used by the hands and face, such as a newspaper,
glass of water, hairbrush, lipstick, gum, telephone, or pen and paper

One person is chosen to be the actor and the other person will be the actor's hands. The actor stands in front of a table with various objects on it. He puts his hands behind his back. The other player stands behind him, so she cannot see the table, and extends her arms out, so that her arms look like they belong to the actor in front of her.

By working together, they act out a scene using each of the objects on the table. The actor responds with words and facial expressions to whatever the hands do. The hands respond to whatever the actor says. For example, if the hands are opening up the newspaper, the actor might say, "I wonder what's in the news today." If the actor says, "I'm thirsty," the hands might reach for the glass of water. The scene can get pretty silly as the hands try to bring the glass of water to the actor's lips since the hands cannot see where his lips are. Continue performing the scene for your audience until each object has been used at least once. Then, let the third player be the actor or the hands while one of the previous players watches.

Scarves

Three or more actors

See how you can use fabric to create characters in this activity.

★ *Props* ★

One sheer scarf or piece of material for each actor

Every player but one takes a scarf. The one player without a scarf will be the character caller. To begin, the caller assigns a character to the other players. Each player then uses his scarf to become that character. After each player is in character for a few minutes, the caller gives each player another character.

Suggestions for Characters Created with Scarves

- Ghost
- Bird
- Old woman
- Superhero
- Bride
- Ninja
- Bat
- Mermaid
- Wind
- Airplane
- Cocoon and butterfly
- Little Red Riding Hood

9

Creative Drama

Creative drama means using dramatic skills and tools such as pantomime, puppets, and masks to create stories, scenes, characters, and plays.

Pantomime is a type of acting where you perform without speaking. A mime uses her body and facial expressions when she acts, but not her voice. **New York, New York**, **Statue Maker**, and **What Are You Doing?** are games using pantomime.

For centuries, puppets and masks have been used as creative drama tools. You can create your own puppets and masks and then use them in scenes. When you put on a puppet show, your hand becomes the character, and you use different voices to create different people. Use your homemade puppets in **The Frog Prince**.

When you act with masks, you use your body, because the mask never changes it's expression. For example, the mask cannot smile, but you can show happiness by jumping up and down joyfully; the mask cannot cry, but you can show sadness by drooping your body.

Get your imaginations in full gear for these timeless, creative drama activities.

> *Masks date back to ancient Japan. The Samurai used masks to frighten their enemies. Primitive people used masks in rituals for luck, to bring rain, and to help win wars. The ancient Greeks were the first to use masks in theater.*

109

One or more actors

Mimes are actors who do not use words or sounds when they act. They rely on their gestures and expressions to show their feelings and let the audience know what they are doing. *Pantomime* is acting without words or sounds. In improv, objects are usually pantomimed because you never know what you will need. Pantomime gives you the freedom to create any object in the world.

★ *Props* ★

Variety of household objects

Practice using objects. Notice how your hands and body move. After some practice, perform for others without the object, but move your body as you would when using the object, and see if the other players can guess what object you're using.

Try acting out the following pantomime scenes alone or with a group:
- Tug-of-war game
- Volleyball game
- Baking a cake
- Working in an office
- Playing in a sandbox
- Cleaning a kitchen
- Walking a dog

See how many scenes you can come up with on your own. After performing a few scenes, switch places and let another player perform while you try to figure out what they're doing.

Marcel Marceau is a mime who's most famous character is named Bip.

New York, New York

Four or more actors

Here's a fast-paced, competitive game using pantomime.

★ Props ★

Room to run

Divide into two teams. Team A goes to one end of the room, touching the wall; team B goes to the other end of the room, touching the opposite wall.

Team A thinks of a job to pantomime. When team A has decided on a job, they let team B know they are ready for the game to begin.

Members of team B take a giant step toward the center and ask, "where are you from?"

Members of team A take a giant step toward the center and answer, "New York, New York."

Members of team B, taking another giant step, ask, "what's your trade?"

Members of team A, taking another giant step, answer, "lemonade."

Members of team B take one more step and demand, "Show us if you're not afraid."

Team A begins pantomiming their job. Team B guesses out loud what that job is. As soon as a player from team B guesses correctly, team A turns and runs back to their wall while team B runs after them trying to tag them. If a team A member is tagged before he reaches the wall, he must join team B. The game continues with team B coming up with a job and then following the steps above until they get to pantomime their chosen job. Keep playing the game until everyone is on the same team.

Four or more actors

In this game you can be a shopper, a salesperson, and even a magic statue that comes to life. Use pantomime to show what kind of statue you are.

In farces characters will often pretend to be statues when they are hiding from others.

Collectively decide who will be the statue maker and who will be the shopper. Everyone else will be a statue. When ready, the statue maker says, "Go crazy!" Each statue begins to dance around, moving and shaking her body every which way until the statue maker yells, "Freeze!" All statues freeze immediately. At this point, the shopper comes in to buy a statue. The statue maker welcomes the shopper to the statue store and shows him around. They stop at each statue and turn them on, one at a time, by touching the statue on one shoulder. When a statue is turned on, it begins moving and acting like whatever kind of statue it is. As soon as the statue maker and the shopper can tell what kind of statue it is, they turn it off by touching its shoulder again, and move on to the next statue.

After they have checked out all of the statues, the shopper chooses which one he wants to buy. The chosen statue becomes the next statue maker. The previous statue maker becomes the next shopper. And the original shopper becomes a statue. Now the game is ready to begin again.

Acting tips for statues: When you're a statue and you're in your frozen position, think about what kind of statue you will be when you are turned on. Use the position that you're frozen in to help come up with ideas for this. For example, if you freeze while lying face down on your stomach, you may want to become a snake statue or a swimming statue; if you freeze standing up with your arms in a circle above your head, you may want to become a ballerina statue or a basketball hoop statue.

What Are You Doing?

Two actors

This competitive pantomime game is for quick thinkers.

Choose a partner. Ask your partner, "What are you doing?" Your partner responds with something she is *not* doing, such as, "I'm eating an ice cream cone." You start pantomiming eating an ice cream cone. Your partner asks you, "What are you doing?" Still eating the ice cream cone, you respond with something you are *not* doing, such as, "I'm climbing a tree." Your partner pantomimes climbing a tree. Whatever they answer, you do. Whatever you answer, they do. The game continues until someone is out.

Rules:

1. No pausing. As soon as your partner asks what you are doing, answer. If you wait too long, you're out.

2. Don't answer your partner's question with anything similar to what you are pantomiming. For example, if you're pretending to read a book, don't answer "I'm reading a book." Don't even answer "I'm reading a newspaper." If you answer something too close to what you're doing, you're out.

3. Don't repeat. If you say something that has already been said, you're out.

Here's an example of how this game might work.

MAX
What are you doing?

GRACE
I'm walking a dog.
(*MAX pantomimes walking a dog.*)

GRACE
What are you doing?

MAX
(*still walking a dog*)
I'm making a sandwich.

(*GRACE pantomimes making a sandwich.*)

MAX
(*still walking a dog*)
What are you doing?

GRACE
(*still making a sandwich*)
I'm taking a nap.
(*MAX pantomimes taking a nap.*)

GRACE
(*still making a sandwich*)
What are you doing?

MAX
(*still taking a nap*)
I'm sleeping.

Max is out because sleeping is too similar to taking a nap. Grace wins the game.

Stick Puppets

One or more actors

★ Props ★

Popsicle sticks (one for each puppet)
Glue
1- or 2-inch-Styrofoam balls (one for each puppet)
Pieces of fabric, approximately 5 by 5-inches (one for each puppet)
Decorating supplies such as buttons, feathers, yarn, and sequins

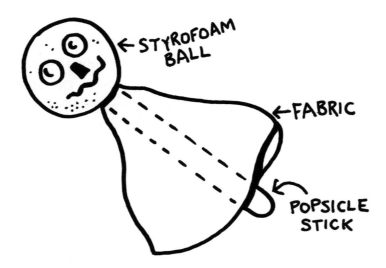

← STYROFOAM BALL

← FABRIC

↙ POPSICLE STICK

 Place the piece of fabric on a flat surface. Place the popsicle stick on the fabric so that one end of the stick is in the center of the fabric and the other end hangs over the edge of the fabric. Fold the other half of the fabric over the stick and push the end of the stick with the fabric on it halfway into a Styrofoam ball. This will be the head of your puppet. Glue decorations onto the ball to create the eyes, ears, nose, mouth, and hair for your puppet. When the glue dries, you are ready to play with your puppet!

Hold your puppet by the bottom end of the stick. Come up with a skit or use one of the scenes in the last section of this book and use your puppets as the performers.

Paper Bag Puppets

One or more actors

★ *Props* ★

Paper bags, lunch size (one for each puppet)
Markers
Construction paper, various colors
Scissors
Glue
Yarn

Place the bag on top of a table with the folded side up. Use the fold as the mouth for your puppet. Use a marker to draw on lips—one lip above the fold and one lip below it, but connected at the fold. Cut out eyes, a nose, and ears from the construction paper. Glue these onto the bag, above the fold. Use the markers to draw on more details, such as eyebrows, or cut out more shapes from the construction paper and glue them on, too. If you want, and if it suits your puppet character, cut out a tongue and teeth to glue inside the fold.

You can make hair for your puppet using yarn. Wrap the yarn around your arm, from your palm to your elbow, five to seven times. Cut the yarn loops at your palm and at your elbow and glue it to the outside edge of the bag. Allow the glue to dry completely.

To use the puppet, place your hand inside the bag and use your fingers to open and close the mouth. You're ready to perform as soon as you decide on a who, what, and where.

Play it again, Sam!

Cut out a body shape and glue it below the mouth of your puppet. Now you can make your puppets sit on a bench or on your lap while you perform a skit.

You can make shadow puppets by using a flashlight and making shapes with your hands.

Puppet Show

Four or more actors

★ Props ★

One puppet theater *or*
one piano bench and enough material to drape over it *or*
one large box (like one for a refrigerator or stove)
with a large square cut out at the top (for the stage)

After you've made puppets (see the two previous activities), make up names for each of them, and decide what kind of characters you've created. Are they happy looking puppets? Do they look sad or mean? Create a voice for each puppet that suits its look. Practice talking with this voice while using the puppet. Next, introduce your puppets to everyone elses' puppets. Let them interact for a while. (This will help you with the next step.)

Divide into groups of two or more. Each group should make up a story that includes all of the puppets in the group. Rehearse the show until your are ready to perform. When everyone is ready, perform your puppet shows for each other. Kneel behind the puppet theater or piano bench, or crouch down inside the box. Reach up high enough so that you audience can see your puppets. Remember to always move the puppet that is talking, so the audience can tell which one it is.

The Frog Prince

Here's a puppet play adapted from a Brothers Grimm story. You can use your paper bag or stick puppets to tell this tale.

★ Characters ★

Witch
Princess
Frog
Prince

★ Props ★

Ball
Two dinner plates

Scene 1: At the pond

(WITCH puppet appears.)

WITCH

Hello. I am a witch, and I love to turn princes into frogs! Do you want to know how I do it? I just dance my magic dance while singing, "Bibbily, babbily, boobily, bog, turn this prince into a frog! Bibbily, babbily, boobily boo, until a princess kisses you." Someone's coming! I'll hide over here.
(WITCH puppet hides, PRINCE puppet appears.)

PRINCE

I'm lost. Have you seen anyone around here?
(Audience responds "A witch!")
A witch? Which way did she go?
(PRINCE looks left, WITCH appears right.)

WITCH

Hello.
(PRINCE jumps.)

PRINCE

Oh, hello. I didn't see you there.

WITCH

Who are you?

PRINCE

I am the Prince.

WITCH

Perfect!
(WITCH dances.)
Bibbily, babbily, boobily, bog, turn this prince into a frog! Bibbily, babbily, boobily boo, until a princess kisses you.
(PRINCE puppet disappears, as FROG puppet appears. WITCH laughs and exits.)

FROG

Oh dear, ribbit. I don't feel quite myself, ribbit. What's happened to me, ribbit.
(Audience responds "You're a frog!")
A frog, ribbit! Oh, no, ribbit!
(PRINCESS sings from offstage.)
Someone's coming, ribbit!
(FROG disappears, PRINCESS puppet appears with ball.)

PRINCESS

(singing)
Oh, what a day to play and play with my ball of gold, truly beautiful to behold.
(She drops her ball into the pond.)
Oh, no! My beautiful ball of gold! It's gone!
(She cries. FROG appears.)

FROG

What's the matter, ribbit?

PRINCESS

My beautiful ball of gold has fallen into the pond.
(She continues to cry.)

FROG

If I get it for you, may I eat, ribbit, and sleep, ribbit, in your castle, ribbit?

PRINCESS

Oh, yes.

FROG

I'll be right back, ribbit.
(FROG disappears, and reappears with the ball.)

PRINCESS

Thank you!
(She disappears.)

FROG

Wait, ribbit! What about our deal, ribbit?
(He disappears.)

Scene 2: In the palace

(PRINCESS appears.)

PRINCESS

The royal chef has made my favorite meal, mmm, delicious.
(FROG appears.)

FROG

Hello, ribbit.

PRINCESS

What are you doing here?

FROG

Did you forget our deal, ribbit? I came to eat in the castle, ribbit.

PRINCESS

A frog eat with a princess? Never!

FROG

But you gave me your word, ribbit.

PRINCESS

Very well. Here you are.
(She hands him a plate, they eat.)

FROG

That was delicious, ribbit, now where will I sleep, ribbit?

PRINCESS

Outside with the other frogs.

FROG

No, princess, ribbit. You promised I could eat, ribbit, and sleep, ribbit in your castle, ribbit.

PRINCESS

Very well, my room is this way.
(She drags him up to her room.)
You can sleep there.
(They go to sleep. PRINCE puppet appears in a dream.)

PRINCE

Princess, I am not really a frog. I am a prince. An evil witch cast a spell on me.
(PRINCE puppet disappears, WITCH puppet appears.)

WITCH

Bibbily, babbily, boobily, bog, turn this prince into a frog! Bibbily, babbily, boobily boo, until a princess kisses you.
(WITCH puppet disappears.)

PRINCESS

(awakening)
I had the strangest dream. There was a handsome prince, and a witch who said that the prince will be a frog until he is kissed by a princess. Well, it's worth a try.
(PRINCESS kisses FROG. FROG puppet disappears; PRINCE puppet appears.)

PRINCE

Thank you, Princess. You have lifted the curse.

PRINCESS

And I have learned to always keep my word. Shall we be friends?

PRINCE

Yes.

PRINCESS

Let's go out and play with my ball of gold.

PRINCE AND PRINCESS

(singing)
Oh, what a day to play and play with my ball of gold, truly beautiful to behold.
The end.

You can find other puppet plays in books at your library such as *Plays for Young Puppeteers* by Lewis Mahlmann and David Cadwalader Jones.

Paper Plate Masks

One or more actors

In ancient times, all actors were men, so a mask was worn to distinguish a female character for the audience.

★ Props ★

Paper plates (one for each mask)
Colored markers
Scissors
Yarn
Glue
Decorating supplies such as buttons, feathers, sequins, and pompons

Hold a paper plate up to your face, feel where your eyes are through the plate, and use a marker to mark your eyes on the plate. Following these marks, cut out holes where your eyes will be. Decorate your mask using the markers and supplies. Be creative. Eyelashes can be made out of sequins or the ears can be made of pompons. Think about the kind of character you'd like to create and decorate your mask to fit this character.

When you're finished decorating your mask, cut one slit on each side of the plate, just below your glued on ears, about a half inch long, and a half inch from the side edges of the plate. Cut two pieces of yarn, each about an arm's length, and thread one piece of yarn through each hole and knot it. Then tie the mask behind your head.

Now you're ready to perform. All you need to do is decide on a who, what, and where, find an audience, and you're ready to be onstage!

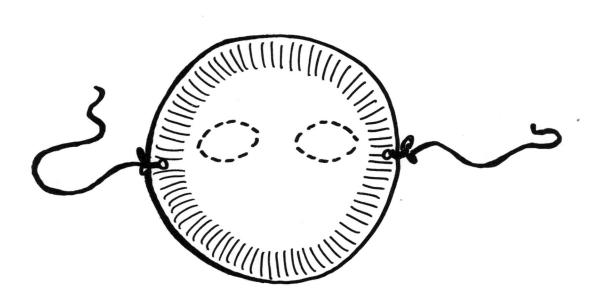

Papier-Mâché Masks

Two or more actors

Instead of a typical mask which goes over your face, here's a mask that you wear on top of your head, like a hat. Because the face of this mask will be turned toward the ceiling, you can portray two characters. When you act with this mask, tilt your head down to let the audience see the mask's face.

You'll need a partner to help you make this one.

★ Props ★

Newspaper
Masking tape
Papier-mâché
Large bowl
Scissors
Tempera paints
Paintbrushes

Place five full size pieces of newspaper on your head. Hold the newspaper down over your ears while your partner runs a strip of masking tape all the way around the newspaper just above your ears (just like where the brim of a hat is) a couple of times. Your partner should put enough tape on the newspaper so that it will stay in the shape of your head when you take the newspaper off. After you lift the mask off of your head, put crumpled up newspaper underneath the mask so that it won't smash down flat while you work on building its face.

Build the shape of a face on your mask by taping more crumpled newspaper on top of it to make the nose, ears, and so on. Once the mask is in the shape you want, place the papier-mâché in a bowl and follow the package directions to mix. Cut some newspaper into long strips. Dip one strip at a time into the papier-mâché mix and cover your mask with them. Cover your entire mask at least twice with the papier-mâché strips. Let your mask dry overnight.

Once dry, paint your mask with tempera paints. Your mask should look like a hat. You don't need to cut eye holes in this mask since you'll be wearing it on your head. When you wear the mask on top of your head, the mask's face should be looking at the ceiling. Now you're ready to get onstage.

Acting with Masks

Four or more actors

Perhaps the most ancient form of theater, mask acting uses the body to express feelings.

★ Props ★

Homemade masks (see previous activities in this chapter)

After you have made your masks, think about the character type each one is. Create names for each inspired by these characteristics. Create a special movement for each mask character. For example, some characters might do a little dance as they walk, others might flap their arms. Put the mask on and practice moving while wearing it. After a few minutes, take turns introducing your mask to the other actors and, they can introduce their masks to you.

Divide into groups. In your group, make up a story that includes all of the mask characters in the group. Turn the story into a scene. Rehearse the scene until you're ready to perform it. When every group is finished rehearsing, perform your mask scene for the other groups and watch the other groups' scenes. Remember to use your entire body to express how your character is feeling in your scene.

10

Behind the Scenes

During a play, you only see the actors, but many important things happen behind the scenes.

One important job is to make the sound effects for a play. For example, if the play is outside, you might use birds, wind, or car sound effects. Indoor sound effects might be needed, too, such as doorbells or telephones. You can practice these in **Sound Effects Story**.

The audience can tell a lot about a character from his costume and makeup. Create new characters based on costumes in **Creative Costume Play**. If you're playing an animal character in a play, you can make the ears and tails with **Animal Costumes**.

Makeup and face painting is fun to do at home or at costume parties or for plays. Use the same tools and techniques as a professional makeup artist in **Stage Makeup** and **Makeup Morgue**.

Next, try your hand at designing a set with **Sketch a Set** and **Set Diorama**. Both activities involve attending a *production meeting* where designers and directors meet to discuss the backstage elements of a play.

Many plays call for props or objects to be carried onstage by actors. **Prop Characters** and **Prop Scenes** will help you be creative with objects.

Once you combine the previous acting games with these backstage activities, you'll know just about everything necessary to mount a full production.

In Japanese Kabuki theater the color of a character's makeup shows the audience what kind of character he is.

Sound Effects Story

Two or more actors

While in the movies many sound effects are made with machines and instruments, you can make most of these sounds by using just your voice, your hands, and/or your body. If you have a tape recorder, tape this activity so you can hear what the sound effects sound like.

Choose one player to be the leader. The leader sits facing all the other players. She calls out a series of sound effects. After each one, the other players make this sound by using their voices, hands, or bodies.

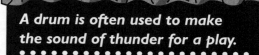

A drum is often used to make the sound of thunder for a play.

Suggestions for Sound Effects

- Alarm clock
- Yawn
- Shower
- Opening door
- Opening dresser drawer
- Birds singing
- Light breeze
- Train
- Blowing wind
- Rain
- Thunderstorm
- Galloping horse
- Walking up creaky stairs
- Doorbell
- Door slamming shut
- Cat
- Witch laughing
- Ghost
- Monster
- Running downstairs
- Motorcycle
- Babbling brook
- Frog
- Cricket
- Splash
- Blow-dryer
- Popcorn popping
- Crackling fireplace
- Snoring

The leader reads the following story that uses these sound effects. The leader should pause after each bolded word so that the other players can make this sound.

This is the story of my scary day. One day I woke up to the sound of my **alarm clock**. I **yawned** and got out of bed. I took a **shower**. When I was done, I **opened up my closet door** and took out some of my clothes for the day. Then I **opened my dresser drawer** and took out the rest of my clothes and got dressed. I went downstairs and **opened the front door**. It was a beautiful day. There was a **light breeze** and **birds were singing**.

Off in the distance I heard a **train coming**. It grew **closer** and **closer**. I ran to the train and hopped on. I rode for a while until it **suddenly stopped**. I got off the train. The **wind was blowing**. It started to **rain** a little, then **harder** and **harder**. It turned into a **thunderstorm**.

Off in the distance I heard a **horse galloping**. It got **closer** and **closer**. I followed the horse to a spooky looking house.

I walked up the **creaky stairs** and rang the **doorbell**. The **door opened** by itself. I walked inside and the **door slammed** behind me. I **walked upstairs** very slowly. Suddenly, something jumped out at me, but it was only a **cat**. I **opened the door** of the first room. I thought I heard a **witch laughing**. The sound grew **louder** and **louder**. I **closed the door**. I **opened the door** to the next room. I thought I heard a **ghost**. The sound grew **closer** and **closer**. I **closed the door**. I **opened the door** to the next room. I thought I heard a **monster**. The sound grew **closer** and **closer**. I **closed the door**, **ran down the stairs**, and outside.

I heard a **motorcycle** coming. It **screeched to a stop**. It was my mom. She had been looking for me. I told her about the spooky house. She said I needed to hop on the back of the bike so she could take me to the park. She drove to a **babbling brook**. There were **frogs** and **crickets** along the banks of the brook. While I was peering down at them, I lost my balance and fell off the bike and into the brook with a **splash**.

My mom took me home and dried me off with a **blow-dryer**. We **popped popcorn** and sat by the **crackling fireplace** until I fell asleep (**snore**).

The end.

A human being makes the sound effects between scenes and before commercial breaks on the television show, Home Improvement. One person creates the sounds of tools, animals, slamming doors, and more.

Creative Costume Play

Four or more actors

★ Props ★

Various items of clothing and costume pieces such as scarves, dresses and gowns, jackets, ties, hats, robes, wings, animal ears and tails, gloves, and eyeglasses
One large box

Fill a box with various clothing items. They can be unusual and shouldn't fit just one character. For example, a cape is a good item, but not Batman's cape because then it can only be used for a scene with Batman.

Once all the costume items are in the box, players should take a few minutes to explore its contents. Players can try items of clothing on until each player has created a costume that he likes. Now players walk around in their costume while thinking about and eventually creating a walk that fits their costumed character. Once every player has decided on their costume and their walk, they walk around and introduce themselves to each other as their new character.

After this mini rehearsal, divide into groups and make up a story that includes all of the costume characters in the group. Turn the story into a scene and rehearse it until your are ready to perform. When everyone is ready, perform your scenes for each other.

If you would like to further develop your costume characters see **Visualization** and **Hot Seat** in Chapter 6.

In Shakespeare's time, the fashions changed so quickly that royalty would often give their clothes to theaters to use for costumes after wearing them only a couple of times.

Animal Costumes

One or more actors

To create an animal costume, start by wearing clothing that has the basic colors of your animal. For example, if you are a cat, you may choose to wear all black, brown, gray, white, or orange. The only other things you need are ears and a tail. Here's a simple way to make your own ears and tail.

Fold over the extra paper and tape or glue it to the underside of the headband.

★ Props ★

Construction paper
Pencil
Scissors
Plastic headband
Tape or glue
Socks
Newspaper
Safety pin

To make your ears, draw your ear shapes on construction paper. Cut them out leaving a little extra paper at the bottom of each ear. Wrap the extra paper around a plastic headband, and tape or glue it on. (If you use tape, it will be easy to reuse the headband after you are done.)

To make your tail, find a sock that is the same color as your animal. Stuff it with newspapers and safety pin it to your clothes.

See **Stage Makeup** (the next activity) to complete your character's look with face painting.

Stage Makeup

One or more actors

You can create many different characters with makeup.

★ Props ★

Makeup base, color depends
on character
Black or brown eyeliner pencils
Rouge, color depends on character
Lipstick, color depends on character

Once you've chosen a character, create a makeup plan for her. You can create a makeup plan by tracing the face pattern on the following page and using makeup on the paper to design your stage face. For most of your theatrical makeup needs, you can use women's cosmetics. For special colors (such as base for animal characters), a local costume shop or theatrical supply store are your best bets.

Choose your stage makeup colors carefully. Make them darker than normal because stage lights make everyone look pale and in a theater, you need to be seen easily from a distance. Design your stage face and try out your makeup techniques at home before your performance. Standing in a room with very bright light, with full makeup on, will help you judge if you've applied enough makeup.

Here are some makeup design tips:

Old Age

Use a darker than normal base and black or brown makeup pencil to draw in the horizontal lines of old age on the forehead and around the eyes.

Youth

Even young people need to wear a light base, rouge, and lipstick onstage so they don't look pale. This is true for both male and female characters.

Glamour

A glamorous woman might wear a lot of eye makeup, bright rouge, and bright lipstick. Nail polish, too, if you have time to put it on.

Animals

Find and study a photograph of your animal. Notice the colors and lines on the animal's face. Try to recreate this look by using makeup pencils and a colored base.

*In **The Wizard of Oz**, the actor who was first cast to play the Tin Man (Buddy Ebsen) had to quit because he was allergic to the silver makeup. Jack Haley is the actor who replaced him.*

Makeup Morgue

One or more actors

A makeup morgue is a book makeup designers use to help them create makeup plans for characters.

> *Laurence Olivier liked to use stage makeup to make his nose look larger for many of his dramatic characters.*

★ Props ★

Pen
Magazines
Paper
Scissors
Glue

Begin by labeling seven different pieces of paper with the following headings: old age, youth, glamorous, animals, hair, facial hair, and unusual characters.

Look through magazines and cut out pictures of people who depict your seven different categories: for your old age page, find pictures of older people; for youth, find pictures of babies, kids, or young adults; for glamorous, look for models and pictures of wealthy or elegantly dressed people; animals can include real animals or cartoons; for hair, look for pictures that show unusual hairstyles; for facial hair, find pictures of men with beards and/or mustaches; and for your unusual characters page, look for people who are out of the ordinary such as superheroes, cartoon humans, elves, space aliens, and so on. Glue the pictures onto the appropriate page. See if you can fill up an entire page for each category.

Sketch a Set

Four or more actors

The *set* is the scenery or background for a play. Before a set designer builds a set, they draw sketches of it to see how it will look. While every stage is different, many have a long back wall for a *backdrop* or a large piece of cloth painted with scenery along with two *flats*, two smaller, flat pieces of scenery placed on the stage. A stage where the audience is on only one side is called a *proscenium stage*. Sketch a set design for a proscenium stage.

★ Props ★

White paper: one piece 10 by 4-inches and two pieces 4 by 4-inches
Colored pencils

Divide into teams of two or more actors. Choose a play or story and discuss the surroundings that are depicted in this play. Think about colors that would help create the mood of this play. For example, if the play is a comedy, you might choose bright, happy colors. If the play is a drama, you might choose darker colors.

Using your colored pencils, sketch your backdrop on the long piece of paper and the two flats on the shorter pieces, one on each piece.

When all the groups have finished, hold a production meeting. A *production meeting* is a meeting where the designers explain their designs to the director and other designers. In turn, every group presents their design, explains what everything means, and why they chose their colors.

To continue your set design, use your sketch to create a set diorama (see the following activity).

The movie Oklahoma was actually filmed in Arizona.

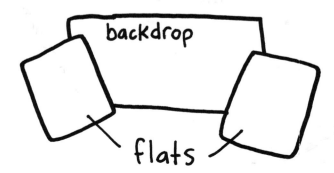

backdrop

flats

Set Diorama

One or more actors

After the director and designer have agreed on the set sketch, the next thing the set designer does is make a model of the entire set.

★ Props ★

Shoe box (one for each diorama)
Cardboard: two pieces, 4 by 4-inches
Glue
Craft materials such as cotton balls, popsicle sticks, clay, rocks, sticks, and pipe cleaners
Doll house furniture
(pieces depend on play)

Set your shoe box lengthwise on a table, with the open part facing you. Glue your backdrop to the back of your box. Glue your flats to cardboard so they are sturdy. You can get your card-board flats to stand by sticking a ball of clay to the bottom edge of each cardboard piece and then flattening it on a tabletop. Place one flat on either side of your shoebox backdrop, angled out so the audience can see the set once it's built. Now add the furniture or other set pieces to your diorama. (What pieces you need are determined by the play script you've selected. If, for example, the entire play takes place outside, you won't need any furniture and you might want to make trees out of small sticks or snow out of cotton balls. But if, for example, all the action occurs in a living room, then you'll need a couch, some chairs, and other items. Read through the script to pick out the furniture you'll need. This is also a great way to create a props list.)

If a number of people have created dioramas, hold a joint production meeting. Here you can show them your work and explain the choices you made, and they can do the same.

Prop Characters

Four or more actors

> *In early rehearsals, the shape of the set may be marked on the floor with masking tape so the actors can rehearse moving around the scenery once it is built and placed onstage.*

A *prop* is anything an actor carries onstage. You can tell a lot about a character by the things they carry around.

★ Props ★

Variety of objects such as a tea cup, stuffed animal, cellular phone, framed photo, whistle, feather, jump rope, briefcase, magnifying glass, and paintbrush

One large box

> *Charlie Chaplin's cane is a famous prop that helped him get into character.*

Place all the props you've collected into the box. All the players can examine the objects in the box until each player picks out one that he'd like to use for this game. Next, each player needs to think about the kind of person who would carry or use this object for a prop then create a character based on this prop. Each player can come up with a name, a walk, and a voice for his character. Once everyone has created a character, all players walk around, in character, and introduce themselves to the other players in character.

Divide into groups and make up a story that includes all of the characters and props in the group. Turn the story into a scene, and rehearse the scene until you are ready to perform. When everyone is ready, perform your scenes for each other.

Two or more actors

Props can be very important, not only to characters, but to the entire scene. Create scenes based on props.

★ Props ★

Variety of objects such as a book, an umbrella, a tea pot, potted plant, framed photo, hanger, whistle, feather, basketball, jump rope, yo-yo, briefcase, magnifying glass, cookie cutter, and glasses

Divide into groups. Each group selects three objects that have nothing to do with each other—such as a hanger, a basketball, and a cookie cutter—and creates a scene about the three objects by coming up with a who, what, and where. Rehearse the scene until you're ready to perform. When each group is ready, perform your scenes for each other.

Play it again, Sam!

Have one person select three objects from the box that no group chose the first time around and, in turn, each group can create a scene using these three props. See how different each of the scenes turn out. After every group has gone, discuss the different ways the props were used in each scene.

Monologues, Scenes, and Plays

If you like to work with a script, rather than creating your own play, there are thousands of scripts to choose from. Your library will have many books containing plays for young people to perform. (See "Suggested Books and Plays" for some specific titles.)

If you're performing alone, try acting out a monologue. A *monologue* is a scene for one actor who is speaking aloud to himself, to another character, or to the audience. This chapter includes a monologue from **Rip van Winkle**, **The Snow Queen**, and **Alice in Wonderland**. You can find other monologues in plays, in a book of monologues, or create one for yourself.

For small groups of actors, there are two scenes in this chapter—**The Tale of Jeremy Fisher** and **The North Wind and the Sun**—that were created by professional children's theater actors by using the **Storytelling Game** (Chapter 7).

For a challenge, theater classics offer comedy and drama. A scene from a classic British comedy, **The Importance of Being Earnest**, gives two female actors the chance to speak with British accents.

The first scene of an original version of **Rapunzel** is included for fun and to show you how you can take a well-known fairy tale and update it.

A dramatic play called **The Cat Who Walked By Himself** is included in this chapter, too. This scene gives you a chance to practice your animal characters.

Finally, the scene from **Macbeth** gives you a chance to practice speaking in verse and acting wicked.

Whether you're performing a monologue, a two-character scene, or a ten-character scene, read the entire play to learn about your character and how the scene fits into the entire story.

Whatever script you choose, the activities in the previous chapters will help you prepare your voice and body, focus on the play, define your character, act successfully with the other performers, create costumes and apply makeup that helps set the mood, and create the scenery to give the play a location and time.

A Monologue

This is an adaptation by Emanon Theater Company, 5050 West Church Street, Skokie, Illinois 60077.

Often, actors perform monologues for the director when they audition for a play. Here is a monologue performed by a character named Jane, but it could just as easily be performed by a boy.

★ Character ★

Jane, age ten

Setting: The forest, on a mountain side. Jane has gone in search of clues to explain the disappearance of her great, great, great Uncle Rip van Winkle.

JANE

I'm on a great misadventure today. I'm solving the mystery of the disappearance of my great, great, great Uncle Rip van Winkle. He disappeared hundreds of years ago, and nobody ever found out what happened to him. They say he went up this mountain and never returned, so I'm up here looking for clues. It's very mysterious here in the forest, but I'm not afraid, even though forests can be very scary, like in the story of Snow White. She got lost in a forest, but luckily she found dwarves, so I'm not afraid. Then there was Little Red Riding Hood. She found a wolf, but she got out all right. Hansel and Gretel got lost in a forest, and they found a witch. Oh boy, I guess I am a little afraid. But that's all right, because I'm a brave detective.
(loud sound heard offstage)
What was that?
(loud sound heard again, JANE screams and exits in fear)
I'm getting out of here!
The end.

Other monologues for young people can be found in the following scripts and books in your library:

You're a Good Man, Charlie Brown by Clark Gesner
Member of the Wedding by Carson McCullers
Our Town by Thornton Wilder
Spoon River Anthology by Charles Aidman
Humorous Monologues by Martha Bolton
Winning Monologues for Young Actors by Peg Kehret

The Snow Queen

A Monologue

This is a monologue from The Snow Queen. *It's been adapted by Emanon Theater Company.*

The goblin can be played by a male or female actor. This monologue requires a few props.

★ Character ★

Goblin

GOBLIN

Oh that Snow Queen! She really burns me up! What can I do to get her? I know! There must be something I can use in my evil box! Let's see, where did I put my evil box? Have you seen my evil box?

(looking around)

Is it here? No. Here? No. Aha! I remember! I hid my evil box under my evil bed!

(GOBLIN goes offstage to get the evil box.)

Here it is. Now let's see what's in it.

(pulling out a stuffed animal from the evil box)

Here's a monster I could sic on her! No, it's too small.

(pulling out a puppet from the evil box)

Ah, here's a scary puppet. I could have it chew her up! No, it doesn't have real teeth.

(pulling out a handful of powder)

Ah, magic sneezing powder. I could spread it all over her and . . . and . . . and . . . and . . . ah choo!

(sneezes powder away)

Darn, lost it! Oh, I've got it! My evil mirror!

(pulling out a mirror)

This is a magic mirror. I know. You've probably heard of a magic mirror before. There was a magic mirror in *Snow White and the Seven Dwarfs*. Let me see if I can remember the magic words to say to the magic mirror. Mirror, mirror on the wall, who's the fairest of them all? That's right. Well, this isn't the same mirror, it's better. Here are the magic words to say to this mirror: Mirror, mirror in my hand, show me evil in the land. Now look in the mirror and see evil! Wait a minute. It's not working. I don't see evil, or anger, or sadness, or any of that great stuff. Maybe it's dirty.

(wiping off the mirror)

Let's try again. Mirror, mirror in my hand, show me evil in the land. Now let's see some monsters! It's still not working. Hey, what's this say on the back? Di-rec-tions. Directions? I never read the directions. Maybe I should. Let's see, it says, "Take one evil mirror." Got it. "Take one evil hammer." An evil hammer? I think I've got an evil hammer in my evil box!

(pulling out a hammer)

"Break the evil mirror with the evil hammer." Oh, but if I break the mirror, I'll get seven years of bad luck! That's OK. I invented bad luck! Now it says, "Scatter pieces of the evil mirror all around. When a piece lands on someone, it will make them evil." I like that! Now I'll show that Snow Queen!

The end.

Alice in Wonderland

A Monologue

This is a monologue from Alice in Wonderland. *It's been adapted by Emanon Theater Company.*

For this monologue, it helps to have an actor playing the white rabbit.

★ Character ★

Alice

ALICE

(enters with a book)

Hello. Do you see what I have? A book! And it's not just any book. It's a picture book! I've got a picture book filled with wonderful, marvelous, beautiful pictures. I love picture books, don't you? I'm going to sit right down here and look at all the brand new pictures in my brand new picture book.

(Opens book; realizes there are no pictures.)

What's this? There are no pictures! How could there be no pictures in my brand new picture book? This is terrible!

(calms herself down)

That's alright, we'll use our imagination. We'll just imagine all the pictures. Like here, for instance, we can imagine a picture of a little stream, and a tree, and a little bunny comes hopping out from behind a tree.

(WHITE RABBIT runs by.)

Did you hear something? It must have been the wind. Now, back to our picture. A little bunny hops along and stops to smell the flowers.

(WHITE RABBIT enters, looks at his watch, gasps, and leaves.)

Did you make that noise? I didn't make that noise. What could have made that noise? A bunny? Oh, I love little bunnies! Maybe I can find it. Here, bunny bunny, bunny! Here, bunny, bunny, bunny!

(WHITE RABBIT enters, ALICE sees how big he is, she gasps, he gasps and runs off.)

Did you see that? That was a big bunny! That was the biggest bunny I've ever seen! No, it couldn't have been. It was just my imagination, once again, running away with me. I'll just go back to reading my book.

WHITE RABBIT

(from offstage)

I'm late!

ALICE

Did you say that? I didn't say that. Who could've said that?

WHITE RABBIT

(from offstage)

I'm horribly, horribly tardy!

ALICE

The rabbit? But rabbits can't talk! That must be one extraordinary rabbit. How curious! I've got to follow that talking rabbit.

(She exits.)

The end.

The Tale of Jeremy Fisher

Peter Rabbit and Friends

From an adaptation by Emanon Theater Company, 5050 West Church Street, Skokie, Illinois 60077.

This scene features a storyteller and sound effects. This play has six characters but if there are only four actors, one actor can play the water beetle and Dr. Turtle, and one actor can play the large mouth bass and Sir Isaac Newton.

★ Characters ★

Narrator (storyteller)
Jeremy Fisher
Water Beetle
Large Mouth Bass
Dr. Turtle
Sir Isaac Newton

NARRATOR

Once there was a gentleman frog named Jeremy Fisher who decided to have a dinner party, so he invited his friends Sir Isaac Newton and Dr. Turtle. He needed to serve fish at this party so he had to go fishing. He gathered his fishing pole and tackle box and put on his galoshes.

JEREMY

Galosh, galosh.

NARRATOR

And his mackintosh.

JEREMY

My raincoat.

NARRATOR

And Jeremy went down to the pond. It was very relaxing, and Jeremy could hear all of the sounds from the pond. Frogs, birds, water . . . .
(pond sound effects)
After a while it was time for lunch. Jeremy made himself a butterfly sandwich.

JEREMY

First take out two slices of bread. Next, butter the bread. Then find a fly, catch it, put it between the bread, and there you have it—a butterfly sandwich. Yum.

NARRATOR

Jeremy finished lunch.

JEREMY

Gulp!

NARRATOR

When all of the sudden a nasty water beetle appeared.

BEETLE

(*chanting*)
Galoshes, galoshes, I like to eat galoshes. Galoshes, galoshes, I like to eat galoshes.

NARRATOR

And the nasty water beetle stole Jeremy's galoshes!

JEREMY

I'm galoshless!

NARRATOR

Well, Jeremy was pretty upset about his galoshes, and just when he thought it was safe, a giant large mouth bass appeared and saw Jeremy's fishing bobber.

BASS

I spy a bobber.

NARRATOR

In one gulp, the large mouth bass swallowed Jeremy Fisher!

BASS

I've got a frog in my throat!

NARRATOR

But just as quickly as he swallowed him, he spit him back out.

BASS

Yuck! A mackintosh!

NARRATOR

The large mouth bass hated the taste of mackintoshes. Jeremy wiped the squishy fish guts off of himself, and went home without anything for dinner. When Jeremy's friends arrived that evening . . .

TURTLE

Jeremy, it's great to see you!

JEREMY

Hello, Dr. Turtle.

NEWTON

What smells in here?

JEREMY

Hello, Newton. I'm afraid I had some bad luck at the pond today, and I have no fish to serve you.

NEWTON AND TURTLE

No fish?

JEREMY

But I do have something even better! Butterfly sandwiches. Take your bread, butter it, find a fly, catch it, put it between the bread, and there you have it.
(*NEWTON and TURTLE make sandwiches.*)

NARRATOR

And they had a fine feast.
The end.

The North Wind and the Sun

This is one of Aesop's Fables that was adapted by Emanon Theater Company, 5050 West Church Street, Skokie, Illinois 60077.

★ Characters ★

Narrator
Traveler
Kitten
North Wind
Sun

Setting: Traveler and Kitten are onstage. Traveler is wearing a coat.

NARRATOR

Once upon a time, there was a traveler walking down the road with her kitten. The North Wind
(enter NORTH WIND)
saw the traveler with her coat on tight and bet the sun

> Aesop, the author of Aesop's *Fables, was a Roman slave who wrote stories from prison.*

(enter SUN)
that he could make the traveler take off her coat before the sun could.

NORTH WIND

I bet you I can make her take her coat off.

SUN

Oh, yeah?

NORTH WIND

Yeah.

SUN

Oh, yeah?

NORTH WIND

Yeah.

SUN

Well, I bet you I can make her take her coat off.

NORTH WIND

Oh, yeah?

SUN

Yeah.

NORTH WIND

Oh, yeah?

SUN

Yeah.

NORTH WIND

How much you want to bet?

SUN

A nickel.

NORTH WIND

You're on.
(They shake hands.)

NARRATOR

The north wind went first. He took a deep breath and blew as hard as he could.
(NORTH WIND blows.)

TRAVELER

It's a little chilly here.

KITTEN

Meow. Chilly. Meow.

NARRATOR

But it wasn't quite enough. So he tried again, and blew even harder.
(NORTH WIND blows.)

TRAVELER AND KITTEN

(getting blown around)
Whoa! Whoa!

NARRATOR

But the traveler pulled her coat on tighter.

TRAVELER

It's so cold.

KITTEN

Meow. Cold. Meow.

NARRATOR

Next it was the sun's turn. The sun came out and beamed down upon the traveler. She shown as bright and happy as she possibly could.
(SUN shines on traveler.)

TRAVELER

Oh, the sun's out. It's getting warmer.

KITTEN

Meow. Nice. Meow.

NARRATOR

But it wasn't quite enough, so she tried again, and shown even brighter.
(SUN shines bright.)

TRAVELER

It's really hot out.

KITTEN

Meow. Hot. Meow.

TRAVELER

It's so hot I don't need this coat any more.
(TRAVELER takes off her coat.)

SUN

I win! I win!

NORTH WIND

I guess it's better to be warm and kind than cold and fierce.

NARRATOR

The end.

The Importance of Being Earnest

You can find a copy of The Importance of Being Earnest *by Oscar Wilde at your library. (This scene has been simplified.)*

In this scene, it's important to know that both Cecily and Gwendoline think they are engaged to be married to Ernest. The two men they are actually engaged to are named Jack and Algernon, but both men lied about their name. In this scene, Gwendoline meets Cecily, who she believes to be her fiancé's ward (an adopted child) or someone he looks after. When she finds out Cecily is engaged to Ernest, she mistakenly assumes they are engaged to the same man. The scene becomes very funny, as they hurl insults at each other, while maintaining their proper manners. (British comedy is full of humor based on misunderstandings such as this.)

★ Characters ★

Gwendoline
Cecily

Setting: Cecily's garden.

CECILY

Allow me to introduce myself to you. My name is Cecily Cardew.

GWENDOLINE

Cecily Cardew? What a very sweet name! Something tells me we are going to be great friends. I like you already more than I can say. My first impressions of people are never wrong.

CECILY

How nice of you to like me so much after we have known each other for such a short time. Do sit down.

GWENDOLINE

Do you mind my looking at you through my glasses?

CECILY

Oh! Not at all, Gwendoline. I am very fond of being looked at.

GWENDOLINE

You are here on a short visit, I suppose.

CECILY

Oh no! I live here.

GWENDOLINE

Really?

CECILY

Yes. I am Mr. Worthing's ward.

GWENDOLINE

Oh! It is strange he never mentioned to me that he had a ward. How secretive of him! He grows more interesting hourly. I am not sure, however that the news delights me. I am very fond of you, Cecily; I have liked you ever since I met you! But now that I know you are Mr. Worthing's ward, I wish that you were, well, just a little older than you appear to be, and not quite so very alluring in appearance. Ernest has a strong upright nature but . . .

CECILY

I beg your pardon, Gwendoline, did you say Ernest?

GWENDOLINE

Yes.

CECILY

Oh, but it is not Mr. Ernest Worthing who is my guardian. It is his brother.

GWENDOLINE

Ernest never mentioned to me that he had a brother.

CECILY

I am sorry to say they have not been on good terms for a long time.

GWENDOLINE

Ah, that accounts for it. Of course you are quite sure that it is not Mr. Ernest Worthing who is your guardian?

CECILY

Quite sure. In fact, I am going to be his.

GWENDOLINE

I beg your pardon?

CECILY

Dearest Gwendoline, there is no reason why I should keep it a secret. Mr. Ernest Worthing and I are engaged to be married.

GWENDOLINE

My darling Cecily, I think there must be some slight error. Mr. Ernest Worthing is engaged to me.

CECILY

Ernest proposed to me exactly ten minutes ago.

GWENDOLYN

He asked me to be his wife yesterday afternoon at 5:30. I am so sorry, dear Cecily, but I am afraid I have the prior claim.

CECILY

I feel bound to point out that since Ernest proposed to you he clearly has changed his mind.

GWENDOLINE

(looking around)
Quite a well kept garden, Miss Cardew.

CECILY

So glad you like it, Miss Fairfax.

GWENDOLINE

I had no idea there were any flowers in the country.

CECILY

Oh, flowers are as common here, Miss Fairfax, as people are in London.

GWENDOLINE

Personally I cannot understand how anybody manages to exist in the country, if anybody who is anybody does. The country always bores me to death.

CECILY

May I offer you some tea, Miss Fairfax?

GWENDOLINE

Thank you.

(Aside to audience)

Detestable girl! But I require tea!

CECILY

Sugar?

GWENDOLINE

No, thank you.

(CECILY puts four lumps of sugar into GWENDOLINE's cup.)

CECILY

Cake or bread and butter?

GWENDOLINE

Bread and butter, please.

(CECILY cuts a very large slice of cake and puts it on the tray. GWENDO-LINE takes a sip of the tea and notices the cake.)

GWENDOLINE

You have filled my tea with lumps of sugar, and though I asked for bread and butter, you have given me cake. I warn you, Miss Cardew, you may go too far.

CECILY

To save my poor, innocent, trusting boy from any other girl, there are no lengths to which I would not go.

GWENDOLINE

From the moment I saw you I distrusted you. My first impressions of people are always right.

CECILY

It seems to me, Miss Fairfax that I am wasting your valuable time. No doubt you have other visits of a similar character to make in the neighborhood.*

The end.

*This humorous insult suggests that Gwendoline goes door to door claiming to be engaged to other women's fiancés.

From an adaptation by Emanon Theater Company,
5050 West Church Street, Skokie, Illinois 60077.

This is a fun play that gives your audience a role.

★ Characters ★

Witch
Father
Mother
Demon Radish
Ogre

Scene 1: Stage left is the house of MOTHER and FATHER; stage right is the witch's garden.

(Enter WITCH)

WITCH

Hello!

FATHER, MOTHER, AND AUDIENCE

Hello!

WITCH

Hello!

FATHER, MOTHER, AND AUDIENCE

Hello!

WITCH

I'm a witch. I can do magic.

(pulling out flowers)
I can cast spells.
(to FATHER)
Cluck like a chicken!
(FATHER clucks.)
I can do all kinds of wonderful, horrible things, but mostly I spend my time tending to my lovely garden. Lately, I have been wishing that I had a child to keep me company. How could I get a child? It occurs to me, are any of you children? Perhaps I could take you home with me. No, I really want a little baby. There's a happy little neighbor couple next door.
They're going to have a baby. Perhaps I could borrow their child for a few years. What I need to do is make them want something of mine, so they'll trade with me.
(rapping)
I'm a witch, I'm a witch
and I really want a kid,
so I must convince my neighbors
they don't want one, never did!
I could give the wife a craving
that will make her ache and pine
for something from my garden
'til she makes her child mine!
I'm a witch, I'm a witch,
so I'm gonna work a charm.
Gonna go into my garden
to my little witch farm.

WITCH (continued)

Gonna grow me a radish,
grow it big, grow it wild.
Gonna grow a demon radish
to steal that child!

DEMON RADISH

(rapping)
I'm awake. I'm alive,
and I'm big, and I'm wild.
Gonna be your demon radish
Gonna go steal you a child.
I'm awake, I'm alive,
Just you wait and see.
Gonna make your pregnant neighbor
hungry for me.

OGRE

Hello. My name is Grumble Bonecruncher, but you can call me Ogre. I'm seven, and when you're an ogre, and you're seven, your dad says, "get out!" so now I live over there. I'm out looking for some friends. It's real hard to meet folks when your name's Bonecruncher. People think I just want to crunch their bones, but I think I can help people. It's just that I'm not so much a people person. Well, wish me luck.

MOTHER, FATHER, AND AUDIENCE

Good luck!

MOTHER

Oh, I'm so happy, we're having a balloon.

FATHER

A balloon? Are we having a party?

MOTHER

Oh, no. I meant to say we're having a beanbag.

FATHER

A beanbag? What are we having a beanbag for?

MOTHER

Oh, dear.
(to audience)
What are we having?

AUDIENCE

A baby!

MOTHER

Oh, yes that's right. We're having a baby.

FATHER

Yes, a baby. I'm so happy we're finally having a baby.

MOTHER

What are you baking there?

FATHER

I'm baking a pie.

MOTHER

What kind of pie?

FATHER

An apple pie.

MOTHER

Oh, that sounds real good, but I'm not sure that's exactly what I'm craving.

DEMON RADISH

You are craving a radish.

FATHER

Well, what kind of pie would you like?

DEMON RADISH

Radish.

MOTHER

How about a raspberry pie?

DEMON RADISH

You want a radish.

FATHER

That sounds good. I'll bake you a raspberry pie.

DEMON RADISH

Radish.

MOTHER

No, that's not what I want. I want a—

DEMON RADISH

Radish.

MOTHER

Rhubarb. Yes, a rhubarb.

DEMON RADISH

Radish.

FATHER

You never liked rhubarb before.

DEMON RADISH

Radish.

MOTHER

I know, but I must have some—
(to audience)
What do I want?

DEMON RADISH AND AUDIENCE

Radish!

MOTHER

Radish! That's what it is. I must have a radish.

FATHER

A radish? Where am I supposed to get a radish?

DEMON RADISH

In the witch's garden.

MOTHER

In the wombat's garden.

FATHER

Huh?

DEMON RADISH

Witch's garden.

MOTHER

In the worm's garden.

FATHER

Where?

DEMON RADISH

Witch's garden.

MOTHER

In the witch's garden!

FATHER

The witch's garden? I can't go in there!

MOTHER

Oh, but you must. I must have a radish from the witch's garden. Go, please.

FATHER

If I must, I shall.
(to audience)
What do you think? Should I go steal a radish from the witch's garden?

AUDIENCE

No!

FATHER

No? Okay.
(to MOTHER)
The audience says I shouldn't steal from the witch's garden.

MOTHER

But I need those radishes now!
(to audience)
Don't worry. He'll be fine.

FATHER

What's the worst that could happen?
(goes into the garden)

OGRE

(knocking)

MOTHER

Come in.

OGRE

My name's Grumble Bonecruncher, but you can call me Ogre. Do you have a cup of tuna I could borrow?

MOTHER

Ogre? Oh, dear. No, I'm sorry, you'll have to go.

FATHER

(going into the garden, said to the audience)
Do you see the witch?

AUDIENCE

No.

FATHER

Shhh! Be very quiet. If she catches me, she'll put some kind of strange spell on me, so be very, very quiet.
(trips on a garbage can lid)
Shhh! I said be quiet. Now, where's a radish? I don't see any radishes.
(WITCH and DEMON RADISH throw radishes at FATHER. DEMON RADISH knocks him over. FATHER takes radishes. WITCH laughs.)
I've got to get out of here!
(runs back to MOTHER)
Here.

MOTHER

Thank you. These radishes are delicious.

FATHER

You don't know what I went through to get these.

DEMON RADISH

You need more radishes.

MOTHER

Oh, these are the best things I've ever tasted.

DEMON RADISH

Radish.

MOTHER

I must have more radishes.

FATHER

More radishes?

DEMON RADISH

Or else you will perish.

MOTHER

If I don't get more radishes, I'll pop!

FATHER

Pop?

DEMON RADISH

Perish.

MOTHER

No, I mean, I'll pollinate.

FATHER

Huh?

DEMON RADISH

Perish.

MOTHER

If I don't get more radishes, I'll—

DEMON RADISH

Perish.

MOTHER

Perish! Yes, I'll perish! You must get me more radishes!

OGRE

(knocking)

FATHER

Come in.

OGRE

Hello, my name's Grumble Bonecruncher, but you can call me Ogre.

FATHER

Hello, Ogre.

MOTHER

I'm going to die without radishes!

OGRE

I'm new around here.

FATHER

Oh, welcome to the neighborhood.

MOTHER

Help me!

OGRE

Thanks. So, what do you do?

FATHER

I'm a baker.

MOTHER

Help me now!

OGRE

A baker? That's great. Ever bake tuna pies?

FATHER

No, mostly apple, cherry, and blueberry.

MOTHER

I must have a radish now!

OGRE

Oh, they're okay, but I really like fish.

MOTHER

I'm going to die if you don't get me a radish now!

FATHER

You know, I think I'd better help my wife here. Perhaps we could talk later.

OGRE

That would be great. See ya.

FATHER

(to MOTHER)

I'm going. I'm going to get you some more radishes. I'll be right back.

(FATHER sneaks into garden.)

Shhh. Be very quiet, I don't want to bother the witch.

(DEMON RADISH throws radishes at him. FATHER picks them up, turns around, and runs into WITCH.)

WITCH

Hello.

FATHER

(startled)

Oh, uh, hi.

WITCH

Come over for a little visit with your neighbor?

FATHER

Oh no, I was, uh, just on my way to the market.

WITCH

To sell my radishes?

FATHER

What radishes? Oh, these radishes? How did they get there? I must have been sleepwalking. I didn't realize—

WITCH

Oh, really?

FATHER

Yes, uh, I mean no. I mean, I was just passing through and these radishes jumped up at me. I almost tripped. You know, you could get sued.

WITCH

You were stealing my radishes.

FATHER

Stealing? Me? No, it's just that—

MOTHER

Help! I'm dying!

FATHER

You see, my wife is pregnant, and says she will die without radishes.

WITCH

If what you say is true, you may have all you need.

FATHER

Oh, thank you. You're kind.

WITCH

But you must give me something in return.

MOTHER

I must have radishes!

FATHER

Sure, would you like a pie?

WITCH

No, I don't need any pies.

FATHER

Well, what do you want?

WITCH

Let's see.

(to audience)

What do I want?

MOTHER

It's the big one!

FATHER

Anything! You can have anything! I must get these to my wife right away.
(grabs radishes and goes to wife)

WITCH

Now's my chance.

FATHER

(to MOTHER)
Here you are.

MOTHER

Oh, thank you.

FATHER

I'm going to finish baking these pies.

WITCH

(knocking)

MOTHER

Come in.

WITCH

I gave your husband some radishes from my garden.

MOTHER

Thank you. They were delicious.

WITCH

Yes, well, he promised me that I could have something in return.

MOTHER

Oh, sure. You betcha.

DEMON RADISH

Give her your child.

MOTHER

You can have our child.

WITCH

Thank you.

WITCH AND DEMON RADISH

We got the child! We got the child!

DEMON RADISH

We got him!

WITCH

Her! It's going to be a girl.

FATHER

Who was that?

MOTHER

Oh, that was the witch. I told her she could have our chicken.

FATHER

Phew. I though you said something else.

MOTHER

No, not chicken, I told her she could have our chia pet.

FATHER

You're sure? You're quite sure you didn't say child?

MOTHER

Well, I'm not exactly sure.

FATHER

Ogre, you were here. What did she say?

MOTHER

What did I say?

FATHER

What did she say?

OGRE

(struggling)
She said child.

FATHER

Oh, no!

MOTHER

I was sabotaged by a demon radish!

OGRE

That'll happen.

FATHER

That's alright. We'll think of a way to stop her.

OGRE

I could help!

MOTHER

How do you stop a witch?

OGRE

We could drop a house on her. I hear that works on witches.

FATHER

Great idea.

MOTHER

Even Ogre isn't big enough to lift a house.

FATHER

Right.

MOTHER

We could push her into an oven. I heard of two children who did that to a witch once.

FATHER

But I've got pies in the oven.

OGRE

She's got a bun in the oven.

MOTHER

Oh, yes.

FATHER

Let's melt her with water.

OGRE

Good idea.

MOTHER

Take your squirt gun.

OGRE

I'll distract her, while you squirt her.

FATHER

It's worth a try.

OGRE

(crossing to WITCH)
Singing telegram for the witch.

WITCH

Singing telegram for me?
(OGRE does song and dance while FATHER squirts WITCH.)
Water? You fool! That only works in the movies! In real life it does nothing to me, and makes my demon radish grow even bigger!
(FATHER, MOTHER, and OGRE exit.)

WITCH

(to audience)
There's nothing they can do. A deal is a deal. All I have to do is wait for it to be born, and the child will be mine!
The end.

The Cat Who Walked by Himself

This scene is an adaptation of a story by Rudyard Kipling.

This scene is written in the style of story theater, incorporating narration with dialogue. This play gives you a chance to use your animal costumes.

★ Characters ★

Cat
Dog
Horse
Cow
Sheep
Pig
Man
Woman

CAT
Hear and listen, for this story happened when the tame animals were wild.

DOG
The dog was wild.

HORSE
The horse was wild.

COW
The cow was wild.

SHEEP
The sheep was wild.

PIG
The pig was wild.

DOG
And they walked in the wild woods.

CAT
But the wildest of all was the cat. He walked by himself.

MAN
Of course the man was wild, too. He was dreadfully wild. He

didn't even begin to become tame until he met the woman.

WOMAN

I do not like living in your wild ways. I will pick out a cave, lay clean sand on the floor, light a nice fire at the back of the cave, and hang a dried wild-horse skin across the opening of the cave. Wipe your feet, dear, when you come in. Now we'll keep house.

MAN

That night they ate a great meal. Then, man went to sleep in front of the fire.

WOMAN

But woman stayed up combing her hair. Look at this bone of mutton from dinner, see the wonderful marks on it. Woman began to sing. She made the first singing magic in the world.

CAT

Out in the wild woods all the wild animals gathered around to see the light of the fire and hear the singing.

HORSE

Why have man and woman made that great light in the cave?

DOG

I will go and see. Cat, come with me.

CAT

Nenni! I am the cat who walks by himself. I will not come.

DOG

Then we can never be friends again. Wild dog went to the cave.

CAT

All places are alike to me. Why should I not go, too, and see and come away at my own liking?
So cat slipped away to the cave, and hid himself where he could hear.

DOG

When wild dog reached the cave, he sniffed the beautiful smell of roast mutton.

WOMAN

Here comes the first wild thing out of the wild woods. What do you want?

DOG

What is this that smells so good?

WOMAN

Taste and try.

DOG

Wild dog gnawed the bone.
This is more delicious than anything I have ever tasted. Give me another.

WOMAN

Wild thing out of the wild woods, help us to hunt through the day and guard this cave at night, and I will give you as many roast bones as you need.

CAT

Ah, this is a very wise woman, but she is not so wise as I am.

DOG

I will help you hunt through the day, and at night I will guard your cave.

CAT

Ah, that is a very foolish dog.

MAN

Man woke up. What is wild dog doing here?

WOMAN

His name is not wild dog anymore, but first friend because he will be our friend for always and always. We can take him with us when we go hunting.

The next night the woman looked at the shoulder of mutton bone and found a big broad blade bone. She made the second singing magic.

HORSE

I wonder what has happened to wild dog. I will go and see why wild dog has not returned. Cat, come with me.

CAT

Nenni. I am the cat who walks by himself. I will not come.

HORSE

Very well.

CAT

But cat followed softly.

WOMAN

Here comes the second wild thing out of the wild woods. What do you want?

HORSE

Where is wild dog?

WOMAN

You did not come here for wild dog, but for this good grass.

HORSE

That is true. Give it to me to eat.

WOMAN

Wild thing out of the wild woods, bend your wild head and wear what I give you, and you shall eat the wonderful grass three times a day.

CAT

Ah, this is a clever woman, but she is not so clever as I am.

HORSE

I will be your servant for the sake of the wonderful grass.

CAT

Ah, that is a very foolish horse.

MAN

Man came home with dog. What is wild horse doing here?

WOMAN

His name is not wild horse anymore, but first servant. He will carry us from place to place for always and always. We can ride on his back when we go hunting.

COW

The next day wild cow came up to the cave.

CAT

And everything happened just the same as before.

COW

I promise to give you milk every day in exchange for the wonderful grass.

MAN

Man came home with dog and horse. What is wild cow doing here?

WOMAN

Her name is not wild cow anymore, but the giver of good food. She will give us warm, white milk for always and always.

CAT

I wonder who will be next.

SHEEP

Not I.

PIG

Not I.

CAT

I shall go there myself and see. Where did wild cow go?

WOMAN

Go back to the woods again, for I have put away the magic blade-bone, and we have no more need for friends or servants.

CAT

I am not a friend nor a servant. I am the cat who walks by himself. I wish to come into your cave.

WOMAN

Then why didn't you come with dog on the first night?

CAT

Has dog told tales of me?

WOMAN

You are the cat who walks by himself. You are neither friend nor servant. Go away and walk by yourself.

CAT

Must I never come into the cave? Must I never sit by the fire? Must I never drink the warm, white milk? You are very wise and very beautiful. You should not be cruel to a cat.

WOMAN

I knew I was wise, but I did not know I was beautiful. I will make a bargain with you. If ever I say one word in your praise you may come into the cave.

CAT

And if you say two words in my praise?

WOMAN

I never shall, but if I say two words in your praise, you may drink the warm white milk three times a day for always and always.

CAT

Don't forget our bargain.
The cat went far away and hid himself until Sheep and Pig came.

SHEEP

There is a baby in the cave.

PIG

He is new and pink and fat and small. Man and woman are very fond of him.

CAT

Ah, but what is the baby fond of?

SHEEP

He is fond of all things that are soft and that tickle.

PIG

He is fond of warm things to hold in his arms when he goes to sleep.

SHEEP

He is fond of being played with.

CAT

Ah, then my time has come.
The end.

In this scene from *Macbeth*, by William Shakespeare, three witches are making a magic brew so that they can see into the future.

★ Characters ★

Witch 1

Witch 2

Witch 3

*It's considered to be bad luck to say **Macbeth** in a theater. This is because Shakespeare's play is full of witches and the title character has a lot of bad luck. The only time you can say **Macbeth** is when you are performing the play; otherwise, actors refer to it as "the Scottish play."*

WITCH 1

Thrice the brinded cat hath mew'd.

WITCH 2

Thrice and once the hedge-pig whin'd.

WITCH 3

Harper cries: 'Tis time, 'tis time.

WITCH 1

Round about the cauldron go;
In the poison'd entrails throw.
Toad, that under coldest stone
Days and nights has thirty-one
Swelter'd venom, sleeping got,
Boil thou first I' the charmed pot.

ALL

Double, double, toil and trouble:
Fire burn; and, cauldron bubble.

WITCH 2

Fillet of a fenny snake,
In the cauldron boil and bake;
Eye of newt, and toe of frog,
Wool of bat, and tongue of dog,
Adder's fork, and blind-worm's sting,
Lizard's leg, and howlet's wing,

For a charm of powerful trouble,
Like a hell-broth boil and bubble.

ALL

Double, double, toil and trouble:
Fire, burn; and, cauldron, bubble.

WITCH 3

Scale of dragon, tooth of wolf;
Witches' mummy; maw, and gulf,
Of the ravin'd salt-sea shark;
Root of hemlock, digg'd i'the dark;
Liver of blaspheming Jew;
Gall of goat, and slips of yew,
Sliver'd in the moon's eclipse;

Nose of Turk, and Tartar's lips;
Ditch-deliver'd by a drab,
Make the gruel thick and slab:
Add thereto a tiger's chaudron,
For the ingredients of our cauldron.

ALL

Double, double, toil and trouble:
Fire, burn; and, cauldron, bubble.

WITCH 2

Cool it with a baboon's blood;
Then the charm is firm and good.
The end.

Suggested Plays and Stories for Kids

Puppet Shows

Plays Children Love: A Treasury of Contemporary and Classic Plays for Children by Coleman A. Jennings and Aurand Harris, Doubleday and Company, Inc.

Puppet Plays for Special Days by Eleanor Boylan, New Plays, Inc.

Puppet Plays from Favorite Stories by Lewis Mahlmann and David Cadwalader Jones, Plays, Inc.

Puppet Shows Using Poems and Stories by Laura Ross, Lothrop, Lee, and Shepard Company.

Plays for Young Children

Just So Stories by Brenda Joyce Dubay, adapted from the book by Rudyard Kipling. I. E. Clark, Inc. Saint John's Road, P. O. Box 246, Schulenburg, TX 78956.

Pinocchio and the Fire Eater by Aurand Harris in *Plays Children Love: A Treasury of Contemporary and Classic Plays for Children*, Doubleday and Company, Inc.

Winnie the Pooh adapted by Kristin Sergel, from the book by A. A. Milne, in *Plays Children Love: A Treasury of Contemporary and Classic Plays for Children*, Doubleday and Company, Inc.

Musicals

Free to Be You and Me by Marlo Thomas, Bantam Books.

Really Rosie by Maurice Sendak and Carol King, Samuel French, Inc.

You're a Good Man, Charlie Brown by Clark Gesner, based on the comic strip by Charles M. Schulz, Random House.

Classics

The Doctor in Spite of Himself adapted by Bernard Hewitt, from the play by Molière. Baker's Plays.

The Importance of Being Earnest by Oscar Wilde in *Eight Great Comedies*. Mentor Books, New American Library of World Literature.

Midsummer Nights Dream by William Shakespeare.

Dramas

The Diary of Anne Frank by Frances Goodrich and Albert Hackett, Dramatists Play Service.

The Miracle Worker by William Gibson, Baker's Plays.

The Night Thoreau Spent in Jail by Jerome Lawrence and Robert E. Lee, Samuel French, Inc.

Of Mice And Men by John Steinbeck, Dramatists Play Service.

Stories You Can Adapt into Plays

Tales of Hans Christian Anderson.

Tales of the Brothers Grimm.

Any of your favorite books and stories.

Glossary of Theatrical Terms

actor: any theatrical performer; refers to either a male or female performer

backdrop: a large, painted piece of cloth that is used for scenery in a play

blackout: when all the lights are simultaneously turned off onstage; an effective technique to end a scene

blocking: where an actor stands onstage and how the actor moves onstage

calling the show: telling the light and sound board operators when to fade or bring up the lights and sound throughout a performance

cast: group of actors in a play

casting: assigning parts and duties to actors

casting call: audition for a show where actors try out for and are cast in each character role

center stage: the middle of the stage

choreographer: the person who designs and teaches all of the dances in a theatrical production; the person who works with the musical director and the director to make certain the dance movements work well with other production elements

costume designer: the person who creates what actors wear in a performance

creative drama: using dramatic skills and tools such as pantomime, puppets, and masks to create stories, scenes, characters, and plays

cross: walk like you normally walk on a stage

curtain call: at the end of a play, the time when an actor receives applause from the audience for her performance

director: the person who casts a play and the person in charge of an actor's movement onstage

downstage: the stage area closest to the audience

ensemble: a group of people who work together for a common purpose

enunciating: pronouncing or clearly saying every syllable and consonant

flat: a flat piece of scenery

follow spot operator: during a play, the person who shines a spot light on the actor who is speaking

giving focus: when an actor does not move or speak in order to give attention to another actor who is moving or speaking

good stage picture: during a play, when the audience can clearly see everyone onstage

house: where the audience sits in a theater

improvisation: (also known as improv) is a drama that is created on the spur of the moment, without any advance preparation; that is, making it up as you go along

in character: when an actor behaves or speaks in a way a specific character would

isolate: to move a specific part of your body while keeping the rest of your body still

isolation: warming up and concentrating on one part of the body at a time; an exercise that helps actors prepare their bodies to move freely

light board operator: person who fades the lights up and down for a stage play

light booth: place in a theater where the light and sound boards are located

lighting designer: the person who creates the lighting plan for a play that simulates the time of day and location for every scene's action

makeup designer: the person who makes an actor's face resemble the character he is portraying in a theatrical performance

mime: an actor who performs without speaking

monologue: a scene for one actor who is speaking aloud to herself, talking to another character, or talking to the audience

musical director: the person who works with the director and choreographer to see that the music in a play fits in with the acting and the dancing; he directs the actors in the music for the play and is in charge of the musicians

object transformation: when an actor becomes an object

onstage: a part of the stage visible to an audience

offstage: a part of the stage that is not visible to an audience

pantomime: a performance without speaking

plot: a story

producer: a person who supervises or finances the production of a stage or screen production or radio or television program

production meeting: a meeting where designers and directors meet to discuss the backstage elements of a play

projection: to speak loudly

prop: any object used by an actor in a scene

props master: the person in charge of getting or making any items carried onstage by actors; sometimes called a properties or props designer

proscenium stage: a stage where the audience is on only one side

set: the scenery or background for a play

set designer: the person who creates the scenery—the background or setting for a play

sound board operator: the person who operates the music and/or sound effects for a play

sound designer: the person who is in charge of recording all sound effects or recorded music needed during a play

stage crew: the people who, during a performance, are in charge of changing and setting up the scenery for a play

stage directions: instructions that tell actors where and when to move onstage

stage left: the stage area to an actors' left (not the audience's left)

stage manager: the person who helps the director during rehearsals; he writes down the blocking so there is a recorded plan of movement, writes the rehearsal schedule, makes sure the rehearsal space is set up for rehearsals, checks all the lighting and sound equipment to make sure it's in working order, and makes certain that anything the actors or director need is available; he also directs the technical people backstage during a performance

stage right: the stage area to an actors' right (not the audience's right)

taking focus: when an actor is speaking or moving, she does it boldly and clearly to grab the audience's attention

understudy: an actor who learns specific parts in a play to be able to substitute for an actor in case he cannot perform

upstage: is the area on the stage that is furthest from the audience

upstaging: when an actor is blocking another actor so that the audience cannot see her

who, what, and where: the three necessary ingredients to build a scene

Bibliography

Barnet, Sylvan, Morton Berman, and William Burto, editors. *Eight Great Comedies*. New York: Mentor Books, New American Library of World Literature, 1958.

Bellville, Cheryl Walsh. *Theater Magic: Behind the Scenes at a Children's Theater*. Minneapolis, Minnesota: Carolrhoda Books Inc, 1986.

Corey, Melinda and George Ochoa. *Movie and TV: The New York Public Library Book of Answers*. New York: Stonesong Press, 1992.

Fink, Bert. *Rodgers and Hammerstein Birthday Book*. New York: Harry N. Abrams, Inc., Publishers, 1993.

Fricke, John, Jay Scarfone, and William Stillman. *The Wizard of Oz: The Official 50th Anniversary Pictoral History*. New York: Warner Books, 1989.

Hay, Peter. *Movie Anecdotes*. New York: Oxford University Press, 1990.

Rebello, Stephen. *The Art of Pocahontas*. New York: Hyperion, Welcome Enterprises, Inc., and the Walt Disney Company, 1995.

Gassner, John, editor. *Twenty Best Plays of the Modern American Theatre*. New York: Crown Publishers, 1939.

Jennings, Coleman A. and Aurand Harris. *Plays Children Love: A Treasury of Contemporary and Classic Plays for Children*. Garden City, New York: Doubleday and Company, Inc., 1981.

Loxton, Howard. *The Arts: Theater*. Austin, Texas: Steck-Vaughn Library, 1989.

Morley, Jacqueline and John James. *Inside Story: Shakespeare's Theater*. New York: Peter Bedrick Books, 1994.

Priestly, J. B. *The Wonderful World of the Theatre*. New York: Rathbone Books Limited, 1959.

Novelly, Maria C. *Theatre Games for Young Performers: Improvisation and Exercises for Developing Acting Skills*. Colorado Springs, Colorado: Meriwether Publishers Limited, 1985.

Rasmussen, Bruun and Grete Peterson. *Make-up, Costumes, and Masks*. London: Oak Tree Press Company, Lmtd., 1976.

Robertson, Patrick. *The Guinness Book of Movie Facts and Feats*. New York: Abbeville Press Publishers, 1994.

Shakespeare, William. *The Illustrated Stratford Shakespeare*. London: Chancellor Press, 1987.

Sitarz, Paula Gaj. *The Curtain Rises: A History of Theater from Its Origins in Greece and Rome Through the English Restoration*. White Hall, Virginia: Shoe Tree Press, 1991.

Spolin, Viola. *Improvisation for the Theater*. Evanston, Illinois: Northwestern University Press, 1963.

Spolin, Viola. *Theater Games for Rehearsal: A Director's Handbook*. Evanston, Illinois: Northwestern University Press, 1985.

Spolin, Viola. *Theater Games for the Classroom: A Teacher's Handbook*. Evanston, Illinois: Northwestern University Press, 1986.

Thane, Adele. *Plays from Famous Stories and Fairy Tales: Royalty-Free Dramatizations of Favorite Children's Stories*. Boston: Plays, Inc., 1967.

Acknowledgments

I'm indebted to the following people and organizations: Stephanie and Joe Albright, Arnold Aprill, Martin Bany, Nancy and John Bany, Barat College, Blue Lake Fine Arts Camp, Fran Brumlik, the Cherry family, City Lit Theater, Geoff Coates, Columbia College, Martin de Maat, the Emanon Ensemble, Leslie Felbain, Dan Gold, Jayme Gordon, Larry Grimm, Amy Harmon, Kristie Hassinger, Norm Holly, Ashley Hugen, Illinois Theater Association, Illustrated Theater Company, Hope Kaye, Sarah Levine, Susie Lindenbaum, Julie Lockhart, Jason Lubow, Nancy Maes, the Mayer Kaplan JCC staff, Laura Maloney, Marionette Playhouse, Terry McCabe, Anthony McKinney, Brad Mott, Susan Osbourne-Mott, Sheldon Patinkin, performing arts campers, Jerry Proffit, Kim Prichard, Laura Pruden, Danny Robles, Lisa Rosenthal-Hogarth, Melissa Rubens, Rick Schnier, The Second City, Shanta, Cheryl Sloane, Klahr Thorsen, Janet Tuegel, Tiffany U. Trent, K. Michelle Williams, Brian Winters, David Woolley, and Wright State University.

Author Biography

Lisa Bany-Winters began performing in community plays at the age of eleven. As much as she loved every aspect of theater, her favorite part was the theater games and improvisation. She founded Emanon Theater Company when she was fifteen years old, and began directing children's productions based on improvisation. Within eight years, Emanon became an established professional theater company with a talented ensemble of actors who, under Lisa's direction, create original adaptations of children's classics through improvisation. Emanon has performed regularly at the Halsted Theatre Centre, the Body Politic Theatre, the Second City Northwest, and has toured to countless schools, festivals, camps, and libraries throughout the Chicago area.

In 1990 she cofounded the Evanston Children's Theater in Evanston, Illinois, giving children ages eight to twelve the opportunity to perform.

In 1994 she developed the Bog Children's Theater in Des Plaines, Illinois, for children ages six to twelve.

Currently she is the theater coordinator for the Emanon School of Performing Arts, located at the Mayer Kaplan Jewish Community Center in Skokie, Illinois where she founded and directs the children's theater, teen improv theater, and the Performing Arts Camp.

Lisa has taught improvisation and creative drama at The Second City Northwest, and to students from Cabrini Green, a Chicago public housing development.

A graduate of Columbia College, Lisa lives with her husband, Brian Winters, in Evanston, Illinois.

Kids' Activity Books the Whole Family Can Enjoy

Big Book of Fun
Creative Learning Activities for Home and School
Carolyn Buhai Haas
Illustrated by Jane Bennet Phillips
Includes more than 200 projects and activities—from indoor-outdoor games and nature crafts to holiday ideas, cooking fun, and much more.
ages 4–12
ISBN 1-55652-020-4
288 pages, paper, $14.95

Bubble Monster
And Other Science Fun
John Falk, Robert L. Pruitt II, Kristi S. Rosenberg, and Tali A. Katz
Forty-five fun science activities created by the ScienceMinders project of the YWCA of Annapolis and Anne Arundel County.
"Eay-to-follow directions. . . . A useful purchase."
  —*School Library Journal*
"Highly recommended."
  —*A World of Books*
"I recommend this book for every parent."
  —New York Hall of Science
ages 3–8
ISBN 1-55652-301-7
176 pages, paper, $17.95

Frank Lloyd Wright For Kids
Kathleen Thorne-Thomsen
A thorough biography is followed by stimulating projects that enable kids to grasp the ideas underlying Wright's work—and have fun in the process.
"Ms. Thorne-Thomsen makes learning about Wright a fun process."
  —Meg Klinkow, Frank Lloyd Wright Home and Studio Foundation
ages 8 & up
ISBN 1-55652-207-X
144 pages, paper, $14.95

Green Thumbs
A Kid's Activity Guide to Indoor and Outdoor Gardening
Laurie Carlson
With a few seeds, some water and soil, and this book, kids will be creating gardens of their own in no time.
"Carlson is an expert at suggesting imaginative activities. Fun, as well as educational."
  —*Skipping Stones*
ages 5–12
ISBN 1-55652-238-X
144 pages, paper, $12.95

Kids Celebrate!
Activities for Special Days Throughout the Year
Clare Bonfanti Braham and Maria Bonfanti Esche
Illustrations by Mary Jones
The significance of 100 different celebratory days is thoroughly explained as 200 related activities pay charming, educational tribute to the holidays, history, and accomplishments of many cultures and many people.
"Includes great illustrations and instructions for activities."
    —*Skipping Stones*
ages 3–9
ISBN 1-55652-226-6
304 pages, paper, $16.95

Days of Knights and Damsels
Activities from the Days of Damsels, Jesters, and Blackbirds in a Pie
Laurie Carlson
"This book helps you experience the era of kings, queens, and castles with more than a hundred easy projects straight out of the Middle Ages."
    —FACES
ages 5–12
ISBN 1-55652-227-4
184 pages, paper, $14.95

Kids Camp!
Activities for the Backyard or Wilderness
Laurie Carlson and Judith Dammel
Young campers will build an awareness of the environment, learn about insect and animal behavior, boost their self-esteem, and acquire all the basic skills for fun, successful camping.
"A good guide to outdoor adventures for inexperienced young campers and their families."
    —*School Library Journal*
ages 5–12
ISBN 1-55652-237-1
184 pages, paper, $12.95

Loaves of Fun
A History of Bread with Activities and Recipes from Around the World
Beth Harbison
Illustrated by John Harbison
More than 30 recipes and activities take kids on a multicultural journey to discover bread and the people who created, cooked, ate, and enjoyed it.
"Loaves of Fun will be an adventure for kids of any age."
    —Judi Adams, President, Wheat Foods Council
ages 6–12
ISBN 1-55652-311-4
112 pages, paper, $12.95

Look at Me

Creative Learning Activities for Babies and Toddlers
Carolyn Buhai Haas
Illustrated by Jane Bennett Phillips
Activities for babies and toddlers that inspire creativity and learning through play.
ISBN 1-55652-021-2
232 pages, paper, $12.95

More Than Moccasins

A Kid's Activity Guide to Traditional North American Indian Life
Laurie Carlson
Kids will discover traditions and skills handed down from the people who first settled this continent.
"As an educator who works with Indian children I highly recommend [More Than Moccasins] for all kids and teachers. . . . I learned things about our Indian world I did not know."
  —Bonnie Jo Hunt
Wicahpi Win (Star Woman)
Standing Rock Lakota
ages 5–12
ISBN 1-55652-213-4
200 pages, paper, $12.95

My Own Fun

Creative Learning Activities for Home and School
Carolyn Buhai Haas and Anita Cross Friedman
More than 160 creative learning projects and activities.
"Handy resource, includes easy-to-follow instructions for many basic art and nature activities, science experiments, and games. Recipes for such essentials as playdough, pastes, paints, and sidewalk chalk."
  —*Skipping Stones*
ages 7–12
ISBN 1-55652-093-X
208 pages, paper, $9.95

Sandbox Scientist
Real Science Activities for Little Kids
Michael E. Ross
Illustrated by Mary Anne Lloyd
Parents, teachers, and day-care leaders learn to assemble "Explorer kits" that will send kids off on their own investigations, in groups or individually.
"Preschool and primary-grade teachers will find this an upbeat, practical guide to science activities for young children."
   —*Booklist*
ages 2–8
ISBN 1-55652-248-7
208 pages, paper, $12.95

Shaker Children
True Stories and Crafts
Kathleen Thorne-Thomsen
This charming book combines two true biographies and authentic activities to tell children of today about the Shakers of yesterday.
"Recommended for upper elementary and middle school grade levels."
   —*School Arts*
ages 8 & up
ISBN 1-55652-250-9
128 pages, paper, $15.95

Splish Splash
Water Fun for Kids
Penny Warner
More than 120 ideas for water fun for toddlers to teens.
". . . this handy volume arms parents, teachers, and day care personnel with a wealth of great water activities for youngsters."
   —*Booklist*
ages 2–12
ISBN 1-55652-262-2
176 pages, paper, $12.95

Westward Ho!
An Activity Guide to the Wild West
Laurie Carlson
Cowboys and cowgirls explore the West with activities such as sewing a sunbonnet, panning for gold, cooking flapjacks, singing cowboy songs, and much more.
"Crafts, recipes, songs, and games teamed with an engaging text will have young readers convinced that they're just having fun."
   —*School Library Journal*
"Informative, well-designed, and expertly written."
   —*Children's Bookwatch*
ages 5–12
ISBN 1-55652-271-1
160 pages, paper, $12.95

Why Design?

Projects from the National Building Museum
Anna Slafer and Kevin Cahill

Containing photographs, illustrations, work sheets, and lists of questions for more than 40 projects, this book will stimulate anyone interested in design.

". . . this is a lively and useful paperback that uses projects to teach the value and impact of design."
—School Arts

"This book is wonderful. I highly recommend it."
—Alan Sandler, Director of Education, American Architectural Foundation

"This amazing book is jam-packed with ideas and information covering a multitude of subjects . . ."
—KLIATT

ages 12 & up
ISBN 1-55652-249-5
208 pages, paper, $19.95

The Wind at Work

An Activity Guide to Windmills
Gretchen Woelfle

Including more than a dozen science activities and featuring more than 100 photos, line drawings, charts, and graphs, this book traces the history of windmills and how their design and function have changed over time.
ages 8–13
ISBN 1-55652-308-4
144 pages, paper, $14.95